Prevention of Cancer

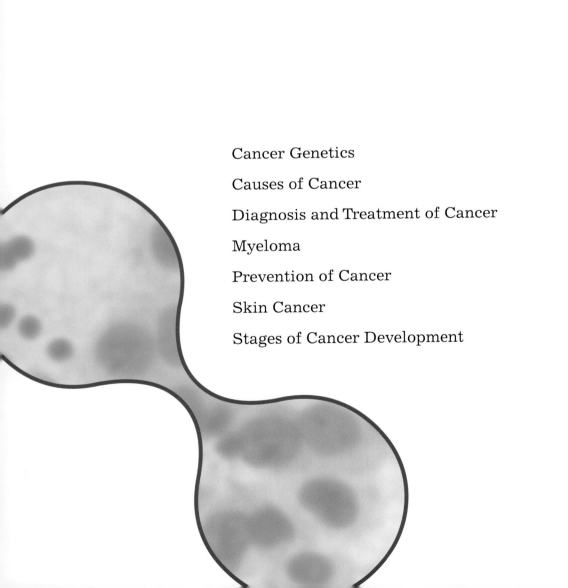

Prevention of Cancer

Robert G. McKinnell, Ph.D.

Consulting Editor,
Donna M. Bozzone, Ph.D.
Professor of Biology
Saint Michael's College

CHELSEA HOUSE
PUBLISHERS
An imprint of Infobase Publishing

THE BIOLOGY OF CANCER: PREVENTION OF CANCER

Chelsea House
An imprint of Infobase Publishing
132 West 31st Street
New York NY 10001

Library of Congress Cataloging-in-Publication Data
McKinnell, Robert Gilmore.
  Prevention of cancer / Robert G. McKinnell ; consulting editor, Donna M. Bozzone.
      p. cm. — (Biology of cancer)
  Includes bibliographical references and index.
  ISBN-13: 978-0-7910-8827-2
  ISBN-10: 0-7910-8827-8
  1. Cancer–Prevention–Popular works. 2. Cancer–Risk factors–Popular works.
I. Bozzone, Donna M. II. Title. III. Series.

  RC268.M39 2008
  616.99'4—dc22

                                                          2007034259

Text design by James Scotto-Lavino
Cover design by Ben Peterson

Printed in the United States of America

Bang EJB 10 9 8 7 6 5 4 3 2

This book is printed on acid-free paper.

All links and Web addresses were checked and verified to be correct at the time of publication. Because of the dynamic nature of the Web, some addresses and links may have changed since publication and may no longer be valid.

Herceptin® is a registered trademark of Genentech, Inc.

CONTENTS

◆

FOREWORD

♦

Approximately 1,500 people die each day of cancer in the United States. Worldwide, more than 8 million new cases are diagnosed each year. In affluent, developed nations such as the United States, around one out of three people will develop cancer in his or her lifetime. As deaths from infection and malnutrition become less prevalent in developing areas of the world, people live longer and cancer incidence increases to become a leading cause of mortality. Clearly, few people are left untouched by this disease due either to their own illness or that of loved ones. This situation leaves us with many questions: What causes cancer? Can we prevent it? Is there a cure?

Cancer did not originate in the modern world. Evidence of humans afflicted with cancer dates from ancient times. Examinations of bones from skeletons that are more than 3,000 years old reveal structures that appear to be tumors. Records from ancient Egypt, written more than 4,000 years ago, describe breast cancers. Possible cases of bone tumors have been observed in Egyptian mummies that are more than 5,000 years old. It is even possible that our species' ancestors developed cancer. In 1932, Louis Leakey discovered a jawbone, from either *Australopithecus* or *Homo erectus*, that possessed what appeared to be a tumor. Cancer specialists examined the jawbone and suggested that the tumor was due to Burkitt's lymphoma, a type of cancer that affects the immune system.

It is likely that cancer has been a concern for the human lineage for at least a million years.

Human beings have been searching for ways to treat and cure cancer since ancient times, but cancer is becoming an even greater problem today. Because life expectancy increased dramatically in the 20th century due to public health successes such as improvements in our ability to prevent and fight infectious disease, more people live long enough to develop cancer. Children and young adults can develop cancer, but the chance of developing the disease increases as a person ages. Now that so many people live longer, cancer incidence has increased dramatically in the population. As a consequence, the prevalence of cancer came to the forefront as a public health concern by the middle of the 20th century. In 1971 President Richard Nixon signed the National Cancer Act and thus declared "war" on cancer. The National Cancer Act brought cancer research to the forefront and provided funding and a mandate to spur research to the National Cancer Institute. During the years since that action, research laboratories have made significant progress toward understanding cancer. Surprisingly, the most dramatic insights came from learning how normal cells function, and by comparing that to what goes wrong in cancer cells.

Many people think of cancer as a single disease, but it actually comprises more than 100 different disorders in normal cell and tissue function. Nevertheless, all cancers have one feature in common: All are diseases of uncontrolled cell division. Under normal circumstances, the body regulates the production of new cells very precisely. In cancer cells, particular defects in deoxyribonucleic acid, or DNA, lead to breakdowns in the cell communication and growth control that are normal in healthy cells. Having escaped these controls, cancer cells can become invasive and spread to other parts of the body. As a consequence, normal tissue and organ functions may be seriously disrupted. Ultimately, cancer can be fatal.

Even though cancer is a serious disease, modern research has provided many reasons to feel hopeful about the future of cancer treatment and prevention. First, scientists have learned a great deal about the specific genes involved in cancer. This information paves the way for improved early detection, such as identifying individuals with a genetic predisposition to cancer and monitoring their health to ensure the earliest possible detection. Second, knowledge of both the specific genes involved in cancer and the proteins made by cancer cells has made it possible to develop very specific and effective treatments for certain cancers. For example, childhood leukemia, once almost certainly fatal, now can be treated successfully in the great majority of cases. Similarly, improved understanding of cancer cell proteins led to the development of new anticancer drugs such as Herceptin, which is used to treat certain types of breast tumors. Third, many cancers are preventable. In fact, it is likely that more than 50 percent of cancers would never occur if people avoided smoking, overexposure to sun, a high-fat diet, and a sedentary lifestyle. People have tremendous power to reduce their chances of developing cancer by making good health and lifestyle decisions. Even if treatments become perfect, prevention is still preferable to avoid the anxiety of a diagnosis and the potential pain of treatment.

The books in *The Biology of Cancer* series reveal information about the causes of the disease; the DNA changes that result in tumor formation; ways to prevent, detect, and treat cancer; and detailed accounts of specific types of cancers that occur in particular tissues or organs. Books in this series describe what happens to cells as they lose growth control and how specific cancers affect the body. *The Biology of Cancer* series also provides insights into the studies undertaken, the research experiments done, and the scientists involved in the development of the present state of knowledge of this disease. In this way, readers get to see beyond "the facts" and understand more about the process of biomedical research. Finally, the books in *The Biology of Cancer* series provide information to help readers make healthy choices that can reduce the risk of cancer.

Cancer research is at a very exciting crossroads, affording scientists the challenge of scientific problem solving as well as the opportunity to engage in work that is likely to directly benefit people's health and well-being. I hope that the books in this series will help readers learn about cancer. Even more, I hope that these books will capture your interest and awaken your curiosity about cancer so that you ask questions for which scientists presently have no answers. Perhaps some of your questions will inspire you to follow your own path of discovery. If so, I look forward to your joining the community of scientists; after all, there is still a lot of work to be done.

Donna M. Bozzone, Ph.D.
Professor of Biology
Saint Michael's College
Colchester, Vermont

ACKNOWLEDGMENTS

◆

My lifetime spouse, Beverly Kerr McKinnell, continued until days before her death to be of inestimable help and support during the labor of producing this book. I thank her first. Portions of the early manuscript were read by the following to whom I am indebted: Tom Clayton, Regents Professor of English Language and Literature, University of Minnesota; Nancy M. Finney, author, Saint Joseph, Illinois; and Debra Louise Carlson, Normandale Community College, Bloomington, Minnesota. It is a pleasure to acknowledge the continued support of Elaine M. Challacombe and the technical help of James V. Curley, both of the Owen H. Wangensteen Historical Library of Biology and Medicine, University of Minnesota. I credit the joint efforts of Chacko T. Kuruvilla and Haudy Kazemizadeh Gol, Bio-Medical Library, University of Minnesota, for steady hands in keeping my computer and me on amicable terms.

Ordinarily the young learn from their elders. Sometimes roles are reversed. Much of what I learned about word processing I learned from my daughter Susan Kerr McKinnell of the Academic and Distributed Computer Services of the University of Minnesota and Public TV's "Tech Talk." I thank her for patience and tolerance of me while I learned new and exotic endeavors at the computer keyboard.

James Chambers, Editor in Chief, Facts on File, made many useful suggestions that enhanced this book. I thank him for his skilled and thoughtful efforts.

I would be remiss if I did not express my appreciation to Suzanne Madison Rohman, who encouraged me with her steadfast confidence in this work. I am indeed indebted to her.

Finally, several young people helped with their support and affection. The omission of their last names should not be interpreted as lessening their contributions. They are Emma, Honor, Arthur, Alex, and Lewis.

INTRODUCTION

◆

Two thousand souls and twenty thousand ducats
Will not debate the question of this straw:
This is the imposthume of much wealth and peace,
That inward breaks, and shows no cause without
Why the man dies.

Hamlet IV, iv, 26-29

I must confess that I never knew what an "imposthume" was, in *Hamlet* or anyplace else, until a truly gifted and insightful English professor, Gordon W. O'Brien, enlightened me. O'Brien, who has since passed away, stated: "in the medical commentaries of the Renaissance an imposthume was more often a tumor than an abscess, and, in the case of the internal (inward breaking) imposthume, the tumor was more often malignant than benign: a fatality resulting from an internal imposthume was almost always judged to be a fatality resulting from cancer."

O'Brien informed me that Shakespeare knew about cancer. Obviously the Bard of Avon could not have been aware of molecular biology, microscopic anatomy, cancer-causing chemicals, or even **epidemiology**—but he got the main point straight. As the readers of this book grow older, they will probably sooner or later become acquainted with someone dying of cancer. That person is likely to die with little outward evidence of the cancer other than perhaps weight loss (known as **cachexia**). Note how accurately cancer was described by Shakespeare, when he wrote, "and shows no cause without (meaning "superficially or externally"), Why the man dies."

But what did Shakespeare mean when he also noted "much wealth and peace"? Consider the former spouse of a vice president, Margaretta (Happy) Rockefeller; Betty Ford, the wife of President Gerald Ford; Nancy Reagan, wife of another president; Shirley Temple Black, child star; and Julia Child, famous television cook. All were afflicted with breast cancer and none were poor. The list of famous women afflicted by breast cancer is long. Famous women aside, consider wealthy Marin County, California, with its many affluent residents and what some have characterized as the highest rate of breast cancer in the nation. Socioeconomic class is thought by many students of cancer as an *established* risk factor, or something that contributes to one's chances of developing cancer. Is this the "much wealth and peace" to which Shakespeare refers? If indeed it is, I bow to his insight.

I respect the immense knowledge Shakespeare had of life, love, politics, history, and perhaps here, medicine. I feel that English-speaking people are not truly educated if they are not at least introduced to Shakespeare in high school or college. To form an acquaintance of significance, one requires more than an introduction; one could do far worse than to enjoy Shakespeare throughout life.

So what does that have to do with this book? Let me make a judgment about education. It is no longer acceptable for an enlightened person to be entirely ignorant of biology any more than it is to be illiterate. Biology is no less a part of the education of a complete person than is an English course. Cancer is one facet of the many sided gem that is modern biology. Therefore students of English, history, art, mathematics, and other disciplines, I plead with you to read and take seriously that which is written in this book. And it goes without saying that biology students are similarly admonished to learn. Become enlightened and enjoy; learning is such pleasure. This book discusses the causes and risks connected to cancer according to current research and how to avoid or reduce them in your life. Careful reading of this book will add to your knowledge of biology and cancer, which is essential for an enlightened person—and it may place you and your loved ones at a lower cancer risk. It is worth the effort.

Robert G. McKinnell

1
YOU ARE IN CONTROL
—WELL, MOSTLY

KEY POINTS

◆ Not all cancer is caused by modern civilization. It is a prehistoric disease that has been found in fossilized remains of animals and humans.

◆ A form of cancer known as multiple myeloma has been found in fossil remains found throughout the world, including Hungary, England, the Pyrenees, and the United States.

◆ Although humans have always been susceptible to cancer, there are some forms of the disease that are preventable.

The message of this book is that in the matter of cancer prevention and risk reduction you are responsible. Not the government, not your teachers, not your family doctor, not even your parents—you alone are responsible. If you wish to remain in a low-cancer risk group, you must behave in a way that minimizes your chance of developing this group of related diseases. As you will learn while reading this book, there are an enormous number of cancer deaths in the United States (well over half a million each year) due in some large part to personal behavior that increases cancer risk. By reading this book, you will learn how to avoid many forms of cancer and become less likely to pay the ultimate price for uninformed behavior. However, you should know from the very beginning that even the most careful behavior will not eliminate *all* risk of cancer. Some cancer is due to heredity, some is caused by exposure to natural radiation, and some is due to chemical causing substances that are yet to be identified. It is difficult indeed to avoid these potential hazards. Even so, most cancer can be avoided.

IS CANCER A DISEASE OF CIVILIZATION?

Many people point accusing fingers at the many kinds of toxic and potentially lethal substances our society produces as the source of numerous ills. They fear the exhausts of powerful diesel-driven tractor trailers on our highways and the enormous jet engines that move our air fleets. They worry about new chemicals that are introduced each year—chemicals from the stuff used to make non-sticking fry pans to the flame retardants used in children's sleepwear. They are apprehensive about the nearly ubiquitous use of powerful weed control chemicals used in agriculture and on the lawns of private homes. They feel that a less-complex civilization would be free of the plague of cancer.

Here at the beginning of this book, you need to understand that cancer is not a disease of civilization. Clearly, not all cancer results from

Figure 1.1   Many people fear noxious chemicals that pollute our environment. Shown here are smokestacks emitting possibly toxic fumes and in foreground an aqueduct dumping industrial waste into a river. *(Linda Bartlett/National Cancer Institute/U.S. National Institutes of Health)*

our modern environment and behavior. Some cancer is a response to factors that are outside our personal control. Let us consider human biology at a time long before the problem of industrial and chemical pollution. Although we cannot go back to that time, we can learn if cancer afflicted people in prehistoric (and obviously, pre-industrial) times. Of course, not much remains of the people who lived thousands of years ago. But in some cases, human bones have been discovered that convey a message about cancer.

A CANCER KNOWN FROM FOSSILS

Multiple myeloma is a cancer of **plasma cells** found in bone marrow. It is a form of cancer that afflicted the ancients as it does people today. Obviously ancient people did not breathe fumes from cars or from aircraft overhead. They knew nothing about chemicals used to manufacture plastics, they had never heard of herbicides or genetically modified crops, and they had no nuclear energy plants. You might think they would have had a tranquil life as far as malignant disease is concerned. But their remains tell us that this isn't the case. So how did misfortune come to visit the ancients in the form of cancer? Quite frankly, we do not know.

If all or most of the ancients who had multiple myeloma came from one place, there might be clues to causation. However, fossil humans who are thought to have had the disease have been found in sites located in Hungary, England, the Pyrenees mountains in Europe, and the United States (including sites in Kentucky, Florida, Mississippi, California, New York, and Missouri). Intensive studies would probably reveal even more sites. Some of the human remains are believed to date from 3,000 to 5,000 years ago. At this point, a skeptical student might ask: How do you know that the prehistoric humans had a specific cancer? Cancer is a disease of cells and no intact cells remain in the fossils. Therefore it will never be known for certain that the bony lesions observed in the fossils were indeed caused by multiple myeloma. However, many experts who have studied the peculiar fossil lesions believe the lesions resulted from this form of cancer. Multiple myeloma cancer cells ultimately cause holes to form in bone that have a characteristic "punched out" appearance. In a progressive disease, one would suspect that some incipient (not fully formed holes) would be present. These are detected by taking an X ray of the fossil bones.

Obviously, the ancients who had multiple myeloma had symptoms other than bones with holes, but only the fossils of their bones remain. Today, multiple myeloma patients often have **Bence Jones proteins** in their urine. It is likely that some, if not most, of the individuals who are now fossil relics had these same Bence Jones proteins in their urine when they were alive. If they did, as experts believe, one might say that this is an ancient urinary analysis made without the urine. While the message here is not about urine from antiquity, it does show how much there is to learn about ancient cancer. What did those prehistoric people do to get this terrible disease? There is absolutely no way that they could have prevented the cancer that ultimately killed them. This is an example from antiquity of a lethal cancer that occurs for unknown reasons. Some contemporary cases of multiple myeloma probably occur regardless of what people try to do to prevent it. In other words, although we know of modern risk factors (such as exposure to radiation), there seems to be a level of multiple myeloma that occurs because of one or more unknown factors, such as heredity or exposure to naturally occurring radiation. The ancients cannot be held accountable for these unknown factors—and neither can people today. That is why this chapter is titled "You are in control—*well, mostly.*"

A COMMON CHILDHOOD CANCER

Another example of a cancer that cannot be prevented with present medical knowledge is **acute lymphoblastic leukemia (ALL)**. It is the most common childhood cancer. No one knows what causes ALL in children. Radiation has been suggested as a cause because of atomic bomb studies. No American children have been exposed to the horrors of atomic bombs. Studies of lower dose radiation are disputed by some.

Chemotherapeutic drugs and toxic chemicals have also been suggested as contributing to the cause of ALL. A genetic component may contribute to ALL vulnerability, but the fact remains ALL almost always occurs with no apparent causation. How could a five-year-old child avoid a disease whose cause is unknown? Of course the child did not smoke, did not work with radioactive isotopes, was not taking chemotherapeutic drugs and did not work with industrial chemicals. How, then, could the child be responsible for his or her leukemia?

Described here are two cancers that are *not* related to cancer risk precautions. The message of the two examples—and there are more examples that could be provided—is that not all cancer is preventable with present knowledge.

A SIMPLE TRUTH: MOST CANCER IS PREVENTABLE

While acknowledging the truth of the preceding paragraphs, the message of this book is that most cancer *is* preventable. Margaret M. Heckler, long time congresswoman from Massachusetts (1967–1982), who became secretary of Health and Human Services (1983–1985) and ambassador to Ireland (1985–1989), stated, "Too few Americans realize the simple truth that cancer is usually caused by the way we live, and its risks can be reduced by the choices we make." She estimated that an astounding 80 percent of cancer is linked to lifestyle and environmental factors. Earlier I wrote that more than half a million Americans die each year from cancer (more precisely, the American Cancer Society predicts that 559,650 Americans will die in 2007—or, about 1,500 per day). The 80 percent that Heckler cites amounts to something like 450,000 *needless* deaths per year! Dr. Lee W. Wattenberg from the University of Minnesota and a former president of the American Association for Cancer Research,

Figure 1.2   Most cancer is preventable. This classic poster supports that view. *(National Cancer Institute/U.S. National Institutes of Health)*

Inc. wrote, "The most desirable way of eliminating the impact of cancer is by prevention." Risk reduction in tobacco smoking is well known. Almost all lung cancer would be eliminated with the elimination of smoking. This has been known for two thirds of a century. Skin cancer is another well-known cancer that is largely preventable. Other cancers with known risk-reduction potential will be discussed in this book. It

◆ CANCERS OF THE PAST

The study of diseases from antiquity is known as **paleopathology.** The prefix *paleo-* refers to something ancient. Pathology is the scientific study of disease. Thus, paleopathology is the study of ancient disease in general and for this book, ancient cancer. Fossil bone is about all that remains of most ancient animals and humans. A few bony tumors have been found in fish fossils that are probably 300 million years old. Dinosaur remains have been discovered from a variety of sites of the **Jurassic** period of the Mesozoic era (during the Age of Reptiles, about 150 to 200 million years ago) in North America and some of these creatures exhibit evidence of benign tumor growths in bone known as **osteomas** and, of greater inter-est, cancerous **osteosarcomas**, which also affect bone. Clearly, cancer is not simply a modern affliction of animals and humans.

While benign and malignant tumors are relatively rare among fossils, the tumors may not have been all that rare in their time. Even now, a wild animal with cancer or any other disease is less able to evade attacking animals and is more likely to be eaten. During geologic times, a devoured animal left behind either nothing, or only minimal fragments which might

is my intent to provide information that will impact cancer in the most desirable way—by prevention.

LONDON AND CHOLERA: A MODEL FOR CANCER?

Cancer is a horrible malady—but readers should be aware that the history of humans has been plagued with many equally dreaded maladies

become fossils. Thus, the rarity of cancer among fossils may not indicate the actual prevalence of cancer.

Modern Chinese males and people of the Near East including Egypt, are vulnerable to a cancer known as **nasopharyngeal carcinoma**, which affects the nasal cavity and the portion of the pharynx that is adjacent to the nasal cavity hence "nasopharyngeal." Egyptian mummies had a relatively high rate of nasopharyngeal carcinoma. We know this because of the great number of mummies that have been studied. Modern studies have shown that the cancer is related in some causal way to infection by a **herpesvirus** known as the Epstein-Barr virus. (The Epstein-Barr herpesvirus is *not* the herpes virus that causes genital herpes infections; actually, there are many kinds of herpesviruses affecting many animals and humans.) It is believed that the nasopharyngeal carcinoma of ancient Egypt had this same relationship to the Epstein-Barr virus and thus we can now estimate the antiquity of a virus through paleopathological studies. Furthermore, we can predict that if ever a cache of Chinese mummies were to be discovered (remember that modern Chinese males are particularly vulnerable to the cancer), they too will likely have cases of nasopharyngeal carcinoma. If this were to happen, it would illustrate the predictive power of paleopathology.

(refer to Chapter 8). One of these dreaded diseases is **cholera**. Patients who had cholera prayed. They did not pray for a cure; rather, they prayed for death. Only death would relieve them of indescribable pain and suffering. John Snow (1813–1858) of London, one of the greatest doctors of all time, discovered that contaminated water caused the spread of cholera. To make one of the most remarkable stories in the history of medicine short, Snow determined that the key to reducing cholera deaths was prevention. Water for human consumption must be free from whatever it was that caused the disease. It was not known then but it is the bacterium ***Vibrio cholerae***, which causes cholera. Snow found that drinking water not contaminated with sewage prevented the dread disease. Prevention worked then and it works now! Few students except those who study history have heard of John Snow or of cholera; that is because this noxious disease has all but been eliminated in developed countries—by prevention. It is a reasonable query to wonder if most cancer could not also be prevented. Indeed it could be, and that is what this book will explore.

SUMMARY

It is true that many elements of modern, industrial society contribute to causing cancer. However, historical evidence tells us that some types of cancer can occur in the absence of these factors. Thus, while we know that we may take steps to greatly reduce the risk for some types of cancer and that prevention may be the best tool in the fight against cancer, it is not possible to completely eliminate the risk of all cancer from our lives.

2

SMOKERS ARE NOT
NECESSARILY STUPID

KEY POINTS

♦ There are more than 4,000 chemicals, including 55 known carcinogens, or cancer-causing substances, in cigarettes.

♦ Nicotine is the substance in cigarettes that causes them to be addictive. There are several drugs, including nicotine patches and gum, that may help smokers gradually overcome their addiction.

♦ Group therapy, antitobacco public service announcements, and doctors' consultations may also help smokers quit or reduce the number of new smokers.

♦ According to the U.S. Surgeon General, the average male acquires 13.2 years and the average female gains 14.5 years of life expectancy by never smoking.

There are many signs indicating that the university buildings I work in are smoke-free. Because the buildings are smoke-free, I often see cigarette smokers standing 25 feet or more away from the entrances (as required by university regulation so that the smoke does not drift back into the buildings). Who are those people? Surprisingly, most of the smokers are health care workers. Health care workers know that cigarette smoking results in lung cancer (as well as a host of other health problems). Indeed, just about everyone knows that tobacco causes cancer. So why do some smoke? Don't they agree that smoking is stupid?

HOOKED ON THE HABIT

It's easy to see why so many people, especially young people, decide to smoke. For one, it's trendy and seems like a hip and rebellious thing to do. In the movies, suave and sophisticated-looking characters are often shown with a cigarette in hand. Add to this the notion that smoking may help control weight or reduce stress. Very effective advertising of tobacco products, peer pressure, and a host of other factors also weigh in. Who hasn't thought about giving it a try? It's no wonder that health workers, who are frequently subjected to stress, decide to pick up the habit.

I was once a smoker, too. I started back in the 1950s during the Korean War. Even then it was well known that smoking was not healthy. However, because cigarettes were so cheap (seven cents tax-free to servicemen during the Korean War; they were a nickel a pack during World War II), we used to joke that we could not afford *not* to smoke. Our chaplains used a big portion of the welfare and recreation fund to buy more tobacco to give away at special events—smoking was a habit that had the *blessings of our clergymen*! At the time, I believed that if tobacco were truly harmful, the government would not let us have it. And so, I slipped into the smoking habit. In too short a time I developed a pack-a-day habit and when I was under stress I smoked even more. I thought I enjoyed the habit and more than likely I did. Smoking was bad judgment, but not the result of a flaw in my character or intelligence.

While it was easy to "slip into the habit" of smoking, it was exceedingly difficult to stop. I quit, but I had a pervasive feeling of deprivation that would not go away—for decades. Ultimately, I won, but it was no piece of cake. So, if you have not started, don't.

LOW TAR CIGARETTES

Low tar, low **nicotine** cigarettes came out during the time that I was endeavoring to quit. A number of my fellow quitters were switching to "safer" low tar, low nicotine smokes during that time—it was thought that smoking light or ultralight cigarettes, while weaning away from the tobacco habit, would reduce cancer risk. That is not true; "safer" cigarettes are not safer. Stephen Hecht and his coworkers at the University of Minnesota found that it makes no difference what kind of cigarettes are smoked with regard to the intake of nicotine and cancer-causing chemicals. His group studied the excretion into the urine of the **metabolic** end products of cigarettes. No difference in the chemicals in the urine of light cigarette smokers versus that of regular cigarette smokers translates into zero reduction in lung cancer risk.

While considering urinary metabolites of tobacco carcinogens, a study by University of Minnesota Cancer Center scientists in 2005 revealed that nonsmokers who inhale secondhand smoke excrete the same end products of cancer-causing chemicals as do cigarette smokers. Further, nonsmoking workers in bars and restaurants excrete

Figure 2.1 Cigarettes of any kind (regular, filter, low tar, low nicotine) are hazardous as indicated by the warning label that, by law, appears on all cigarette packaging. *(Bill Branso/National Cancer Institute/U.S. National Institutes of Health)*

four to six times more of the noxious chemicals than do nonsmoking workers in other smoking-permitted workplaces. The scientists could even tell what days were workdays versus days not worked by examining urine samples.

The Minnesota Cancer Center workers reported in 2006 that another group of nonsmokers were inhaling significant amounts of tobacco smoke and excreting in their urine the same tobacco metabolites as smokers. This group of nonsmokers did not complain—in fact, they *could not* complain. The group was newborn infants and babies of parents that smoked. Incredibly, the level of tobacco metabolites was similar to levels found in adult smokers. It is my opinion these babies were *abused* by the neglect of thoughtless parental smokers. In time, some group of scientists will discover the health effects of exposure of babies to secondhand smoke—by that time, it will be too late to reverse the ill effects.

HOW DOES TOBACCO KILL?

I taught a college course on the biology of cancer for 30 years. From time to time I was asked how smoking causes cancer. That should be an easy question to answer with all of the research that has gone into the study of tobacco. Actually, it is far from simple. Let us begin with nicotine. Nicotine does *not* cause cancer so why begin with it? Nicotine is addictive and therein is a great problem. Nicotine forces the smoker to smoke more and more and makes it nearly impossible to quit. The smoker inhales increasingly greater amounts of tobacco smoke, which contains at least 4,000 chemicals, 55 of which are *known* carcinogens, or cancer-causing substances (listed by the International Agency for Research on Cancer, a part of the World Health Organization located in Lyon, France). The known carcinogens and their metabolic products cause cancer, by, among other ways, bonding with DNA directly to interfere with proper cell metabolism or by forming mutations to the genetic material of DNA, which in turn causes cancer. In a sense, it does not make much difference which carcinogen causes cancer in you or your friends, the end result is tobacco-caused cancer.

SMOKING IS DEADLY

In 1951, Sir Richard Doll, knighted by Queen Elizabeth II for his monumental research on smoking among British doctors, began a

prospective study on the effects of tobacco. This means that Doll's investigation of cigarette smokers was designed to follow participants forward in time, rather than retrospectively. The study, which continues to this day, has identified some surprising facts about smoking. One is that lung cancer and its companion **chronic obstructive pulmonary disease (COPD)**, a disease of the airways, account for only about a quarter of the "excess mortality" among smokers. Excess mortality relates to premature deaths that would *not* have occurred had the participants not smoked. What caused the other 75 percent? One-quarter of the excess deaths are attributable to **coronary heart disease**, damage to the heart as a result of reduced blood supply. The remaining half of the excess deaths are due to other cancers (these include cancers of the lips, mouth, esophagus, larynx, pharynx, stomach, pancreas, cervix, kidney, stomach, bladder, colorectal cancer, and acute myeloid leukemia), other respiratory diseases, and other vascular disease. While it is common to think of lung cancer first when considering the ill effects of smoking, actually lung cancer accounts for but a fraction of the total deaths caused by tobacco smoke inhalation.

The annual total of *unnecessary early* deaths in the United States due to smoking is calculated to be about 438,000 (1997–2001 data from the Centers for Disease Control and Prevention [CDC], a government agency). In comparison, **AIDS** is thought to have claimed the lives of 17,000 Americans in 1998 (2005 Data from the CDC). Thus, smoking-related deaths are 25 times more common than deaths due to AIDS. Smoking related deaths claim about 10 times as many deaths as breast cancer. (In 2007, 40,460 women are expected to die of breast cancer, according to American Cancer Society data). Any unnecessary death, be it by accident, war, AIDS, or whatever, is dreadful. It is not the purpose of this discussion of numbers to minimize one lethal condition compared with another. Rather, the numbers given here are to hammer home the incredible cost in lives lost due to tobacco use.

Although lung cancer deaths account for only a fraction of total deaths due to smoking, lung cancer however does cause over 30 percent of deaths due to malignancy among males. To give some perspective, lung cancer kills more men than prostate, kidney, colon, rectal, all forms of leukemia and pancreatic cancers put together. Lung cancer is the most common cause of death by cancer of both men and women. Sir Richard Doll has stated that about half of all cigarette smokers will be killed by their habit. Writing elsewhere, I state that there is no procedure in surgery, radiation, chemotherapy, or any combination thereof, available now or even rationally hoped for in the future, that could come close to doing more to reduce cancer deaths than simply quitting smoking. Cancer research is extraordinarily expensive—smoking cessation not only costs nothing, but it would also saves an incredible number of lives. It also saves money lost to time away from jobs, as well as the expense of prescription drugs, hospital and nursing home care, disability costs, and of course, the cost of premature end-of-life expenses such as cremation and burial.

A good high school student is wise to be skeptical. The wise student may be inclined to doubt the importance of cancer deaths, thinking, "We all die sometime and thus, who cares *how* we die?" True we all die, but is the notion of not caring how and when wise?

The CDC has calculated that cigarette smoking by citizens of the United States results in 5.5 million years of potential life lost annually. How does that translate into years of life lost to individuals? Sir Richard Doll did the math. People 25 to 34 years of age who stop smoking at that age gain 10 years of life expectancy. (Note: If you are 16 years old now, 10 years is all the time you have enjoyed since the first grade—*not* a trivial span of time.) A lifetime smoker 60 years of age gains three

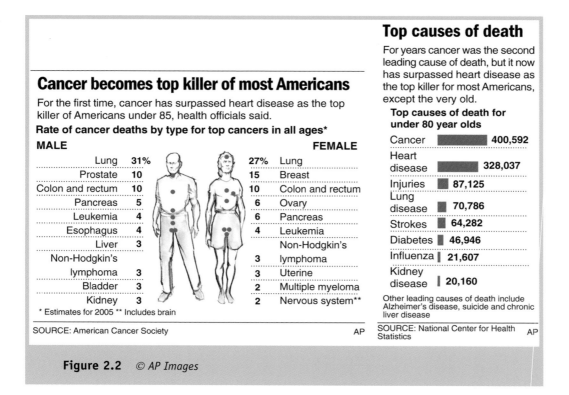

Cancer becomes top killer of most Americans

For the first time, cancer has surpassed heart disease as the top killer of Americans under 85, health officials said.

Rate of cancer deaths by type for top cancers in all ages*

MALE				FEMALE
Lung	31%		27%	Lung
Prostate	10		15	Breast
Colon and rectum	10		10	Colon and rectum
Pancreas	5		6	Ovary
Leukemia	4		6	Pancreas
Esophagus	4		4	Leukemia
Liver	3			Non-Hodgkin's
Non-Hodgkin's			3	lymphoma
lymphoma	3		3	Uterine
Bladder	3		2	Multiple myeloma
Kidney	3		2	Nervous system**

* Estimates for 2005 ** Includes brain

SOURCE: American Cancer Society   AP

Top causes of death

For years cancer was the second leading cause of death, but it now has surpassed heart disease as the top killer for most Americans, except the very old.

Top causes of death for under 80 year olds

Cancer	400,592
Heart disease	328,037
Injuries	87,125
Lung disease	70,786
Strokes	64,282
Diabetes	46,946
Influenza	21,607
Kidney disease	20,160

Other leading causes of death include Alzheimer's disease, suicide and chronic liver disease

SOURCE: National Center for Health Statistics   AP

Figure 2.2   © AP Images

years by quitting. The Surgeon General of the United States writes that the average male acquires 13.2 years and the average female gains 14.5 years by never smoking. I quit when I was in my 30s. If I am average, my gain in life expectancy from quitting smoking has made the difference of seeing my grandchildren grow. I do not want to check out just yet. Life is simply too good to give up. Ask any grandpa how much fun it is to take a grandchild fishing and you will get the same answer, as you likely will from the grandchild. I hope readers agree with me that an extra 10 or more years of life is worth quitting or never smoking.

TAX ON TOBACCO—CHEAP

Smoking is the principal cause of premature death in the United States but, if the lethal aspects of smoking are insufficient to attract attention, consider the fact that for every pack of cigarettes sold per year, there are costs not covered by taxes. Those costs are smoking-caused health care expenses and lost productivity which has been calculated to be an average of $7.18 per pack smoked but as high as $11.25 per pack in the District of Columbia (data from the U.S. Centers for Disease Control and Prevention). Direct medical expenses due to smoking in Illinois in 2004 was an astonishing $4.11 billion. Our country spent $75 billion in direct medical costs to which must be added $92 billion in lost productivity for a total of $167 billion in *annual* health related loss due to smoking. This leads to an inescapable conclusion that tobacco taxes are cheap and that the nonsmoking public subsidizes (and thus inadvertently encourages) smoking. Is it ethical not to collect money that would offset expenses directly related to the effects of smoking? The economic costs, published by the U.S. Centers for Disease Control and Prevention are real. However, one aspect of smoking actually saves the taxpayer money. Social Security benefits are not paid to dead individuals and because smokers have a reduced life expectancy, they are actually helping the nation pay for retirement. A nongovernmental source has stated that premature death saves the government 32 cents per pack sold and this with an average of 53 cents of tax imposed per pack on cigarettes "profits" the government by 85 cents per pack sold. Obviously the government is not profiting when the high cost of smoking is factored into the equation.

LUNG CANCER ALSO TARGETS THE BRAIN

Metastasis refers to the spread of cancer. Cancer is rarely a localized disease. Instead, it spreads throughout the body. This is what makes cancer such a difficult disease to treat. A surprising bit of medical lore relates to the fact that physicians often order a chest X ray when a patient shows symptoms of a cancer in the brain. Why look at the chest? The answer is that cancer seldom metastasizes randomly; rather the malignant cancer cells tend to spread to specific tissues or organs. The brain is one of those organs that lung cancer cells particularly like and consequently, when symptoms appear that suggest a brain cancer, it is possible that the patient has lung cancer. Remember lung cancer cells that home for one's brain the next time you inhale on a cigarette deeply—is that last drag (or any drag) on a butt worth it?

NICOTIANA TABACUM, KING JAMES, A NEW ORLEANS SURGEON, AND SEX

Most people are aware of the New World origin of tobacco. Pre-Columbian Native Americans consumed burning tobacco for religious purposes. That consumption was noted by explorers who took tobacco seeds and leaves back to Europe. In 1556, Jean Nicot de Villemain, the French ambassador to Lisbon, sent tobacco to the court of Catherine de Médicis, queen of France. The ambassador's name was given to this plant, *Nicotiana*. Only nine years later, Sir Walter Raleigh was reputed to have introduced tobacco to England during the reign of Elizabeth I (1558–1603). James I of England (who was also James VI of Scotland and is the "James" of the biblical King James Version) followed Elizabeth on the throne and he reigned from 1603 to 1625. James put the first tobacco tax in place. His tax was a 400-year head

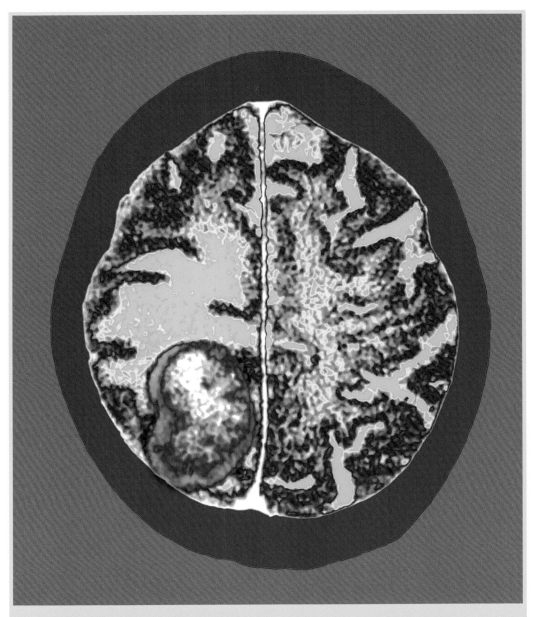

Figure 2.3   Colored computed tomography scan of the head of a patient with brain cancer that metastasized from a carcinoma in a lung. *(© DU CANE MEDICAL IMAGING LTD/Photo Researchers, Inc.)*

start on the recognition that taxes (and therefore prices) affect consumption. He hated tobacco and wrote in 1604 that smoking was: "A custome lothsome to the eye, hateful to the Nose, harmefull to the

♦ WHAT IS METASTASIS?

Metastasis is what both physicians and patients fear—it absolutely defines a growth as malignant. The practical significance of metastasis is that prior to that event, simple removal of the growth is all that is needed for permanent cure. Metastatic cancer is a problem of a far more dangerous nature. For metastasis to occur, the original cancer (known as the "primary" cancer) must grow, invade normal nearby tissue, and gain access to a blood or lymph vessel, circulate in the blood or lymph, exit the vessel and move into new tissue where the cancer cells grow and form "secondary" colonies. The whole process is repeated again and again until there are multiple metastatic cancer growths.

A surgeon can remove a primary cancer from virtually any part of the body. Removal of all multiple metastatic colonies at diverse locations throughout the body is ordinarily an impossible task. If untreated, the multiple cancer growths will lead to the death of the victim. This is why metastasis is justly feared.

Normal cells ordinarily do not move about in the body. Normal brain tissue remains in the brain and normal liver cells remain in the liver. Some noncancerous cells do however move about during embryonic development and adult life. Sex cells do not have their origin in the ovaries and the testes. During embryological development, the embryonic sex cells migrate to the appropriate sex organ. This normal cell behavior mimics to a limited

braine, daungerous to the Lungs, and in the blacke stinking fume thereof, nearest resembling the horrible Stigian smoke of the pit that is bottomelesse."

degree metastasis. Some women suffer from endometriosis, a non-malignant but inappropriate wandering of uterine cells to a distant location in the abdomen. While the uterine cells that wander are not normal, neither are they cancer. Such examples may provide cancer researchers with clues to the cell mechanisms of metastatic behavior. The clues may lead to the eventual control of metastasis—which is the control of cancer itself.

Chemotherapy, the use of chemicals to fight cancer, is a treatment that recognizes that cancer is rarely a localized disease. Chemotherapeutic drugs are given that treat cancer at its many locations in the body. Chemotherapy thus is treatment of metastasis.

As described in another chapter, malignant melanoma has the potential to metastasize, just like lung cancer can metastasize to the brain's tissues. The establishment of metastatic melanoma colonies can occur in essentially every tissue and organ in the body. Common sites of early melanoma metastasis include skin, connective tissue under the skin, and lymph nodes.

Early diagnosis for any cancer is extraordinarily important. It has been estimated that most, perhaps three out of four, cancers have already undergone metastasis at the time of initial diagnosis. As indicated above, metastatic cancer is far more difficult to treat than the simple surgical removal of a localized lump. A monthly check of moles and other "spots" may increase awareness of skin cancer and perhaps lead to an early lifesaving diagnosis by a dermatologist.

Much more recently than the time of King James, Alton Ochsner of Tulane University in New Orleans, became interested in lung cancer. His interests developed after World War I when veterans of the war developed lung cancer. Ochsner was far ahead of his medical profession and scientists when he argued for prevention—his view was do not smoke but if you do smoke, stop now. Prevention was preached by Ochsner and it is as critically important now as it was 50 years ago. Tulane University's surgeon was truly one of the great doctors of the 20th century. Fast forward to *The Health Consequences of Smoking: A Report of the Surgeon General*, which was published in 2004. This report confirmed the findings of Alton Ochsner and Sir Richard Doll.

The issue to be discussed at this point is how to assist in smoking cessation. The lifelong nonsmoker already has an enhanced life expectancy. What can we do to assist those who consume tobacco to quit?

◆ SMOKING—MORE CONCERNS THAN CANCER

Supplementary to a concern for cancer is the following, which is addressed to young male readers: This addendum is in italics and is separated from the main part of the chapter because, while it is extra material deserving of contemplation, it does not concern cancer and the Surgeon General of the United States cautions that conclusive evidence is not yet available. However, there is emerging evidence from careful studies in the United States, England, Iran, Italy, Egypt, Finland, and other places, that smoking contributes to, or may cause, erectile dysfunction. If not cancer, perhaps erectile problems may elicit concern. Enough said?

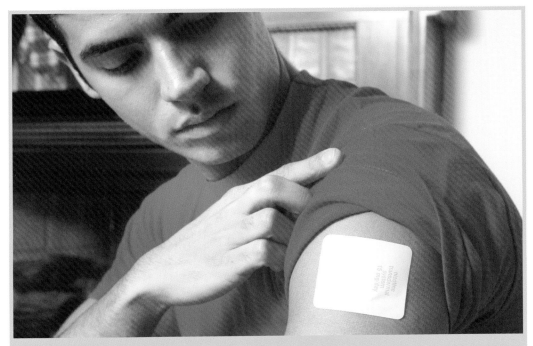

Figure 2.4   A man wearing a nicotine patch designed to control cravings for nicotine and help with smoking cessation. (© *Doug Martin/Photo Researchers, Inc.*)

SMOKING CESSATION:
PREVENTIVE MEDICINE'S MOST DIFFICULT AREA

Starting smoking is easy—it is extraordinarily difficult to quit. The success rate is low and **recidivism** (meaning to "fall back" or relapse) is high. Obviously, epidemiologists and physicians have a lot to learn about what helps a smoker quit. I believe that smokers will profit from direct discussions with their doctor. If you smoke, there are several ways to help you quit the habit.

Group Programs to Help in Smoking Cessation

Individual counseling yields few quitters. However, group counseling is often effective. Groups provide mutual support for those who wish to quit smoking.

In one smoking cessation study, a group of high school students were offered weekly discussions of smoking problems. The students were shown videos and had the opportunity to talk with a doctor about their addiction. They became aware of how much others in their group wanted to quit. They discussed the smoking habits of their friends and parents and how to obtain support for quitting. The students were taught how to manage their desire to smoke and the stresses and social consequences of quitting. They were offered a drug (*with parental permission*—the drug, bupropion, discussed on the following page) to assist in smoking cessation. These approaches were tailored to the needs of individual students. Was the program a success? Only a little more than a quarter of the students quit, but that quit rate is actually high. Worthy of mention is that two-thirds of the students who continued to smoke reduced their tobacco consumption.

Nicotine to Assist in Smoking Cessation

Nicotine has been likened to cocaine or heroin in its addictive power. Because the goal is to eliminate nicotine intake, it may seem odd that nicotine is used to assist in quitting. The rationale is to use nicotine to combat withdrawal symptoms that occur when a smoker stops. When smokers quit "cold turkey," an intense desire or craving for a cigarette occurs, which may be accompanied by irritability and anxiety. As a result, it is better to taper off and quit.

Carefully controlled doses of nicotine can be helpful in enduring difficulties of withdrawal. Nicotine chewing gum and **transdermal** patches that transfer the drug through the skin are well known options for smokers who want to quit. Hard candy with nicotine (also known as lozenges or troches) is also available. These sources of nicotine are available over the counter (no prescription required) at drugstores. However, consult with your doctor before using of any of these nicotine products. They are potentially dangerous with powerful side effects of their own if not properly used. A prescription from a physician *is* necessary to obtain inhalers or nasal sprays containing nicotine.

Another drug used alone or with nicotine replacement therapy is bupropion. Bupropion is a popular **antidepressant**, and is sold under several trademarked names. The drug has potentially dangerous side effects for young people and, like all prescription drugs, it must be used only under the direct care of a doctor. Buspirone and a similar drug, nortriptyline, reduce the uneasy feelings associated with smoking withdrawal, but probably have little direct effect in helping smokers quit. (Buspirone hydrochloride and nortriptyline are also generic nonproprietary names.)

As stated above, the efficacy of drugs in the management of smoking cessation is not outstanding. The majority of treated individuals will resume smoking.

PUBLIC EFFORTS TO AID IN SMOKING CESSATION

Most young people, as well as many adults, have limited money. It was stated previously in this chapter that cigarette taxes are indeed cheap. Many experts believe that a significant increase in both federal and state taxes on cigarettes will reduce cigarette consumption. Many people consider cigarette taxes fair despite their unpopularity. The taxes are unpopular because they increase the cost of cigarettes but fair because

◆ A BOY WITH A MODEST ORIGIN
BECOMES A MEDICAL HERO

The boy referred to here was born Monday, May 4, 1896, at Kimball, South Dakota, and was named Edward William Alton Ochsner, although he was far better known as simply Alton Ochsner. After growing up in Kimball, Ochsner worked his way through the University of South Dakota and graduated in 1918 with a near A average. He was inducted into Phi Beta Kappa, the highest academic honorary society on campus. This was followed by medical training at Washington University in Saint Louis, Missouri. Before long, he was a 30-year-old surgeon teaching at the University of Wisconsin in Madison, which was soon followed by an invitation to become head, at age 31, of the Department of Surgery, Tulane University, New Orleans, Louisiana. While he was an extraordinarily gifted surgeon (he was cofounder and long time coeditor of the medical journal *Surgery* with University of Minnesota's Owen Wangensteen), he is remembered here because of his pioneering efforts devoted to education about the hazards of smoking. Dr. Ochsner wrote:

> When I was a medical student in 1919, we admitted a patient with lung cancer to Barnes (hospital in Saint Louis). As usual, the patient died, because the mortality was about 100 percent. Dr. Dock (a medical school professor) had us witness the autopsy because he said that the condition was so rare that we'd never see another case for as long as we lived. I didn't see another case for 17 years—until 1936. Then there were nine cases in six months. An epidemic. There had to be a cause. They were all men, all smoked cigarettes heavily, all began smoking in the First World War. When I researched the history

Figure 2.5   Alton Ochsner was a pioneer in establishing the link between smoking and lung cancer. *(National Library of Medicine/U.S. National Institutes of Health)*

of smoking, I found that very few cigarettes had been consumed prior to World War I. In 1936, I had the temerity to state—not suggest—that cigarettes caused this new plague.

In 1939, Alton Ochsner repeated his view on the cause of lung cancer: "It's our conviction that the increase in the incidence of pulmonary carcinoma is due largely to the increase in smoking, particularly cigarette smoking, which is universally associated with inhalation."

(continues)

(continued)

Few believed the New Orleans surgeon. Dr. Evarts A. Graham, professor of surgery at Washington University School of Medicine, a 50-year smoker himself, simply viewed Ochsner's notion as "how dumb and how stupid." Dr. Graham thought of the relationship between smoking and lung cancer as coincidental and remarked that the sale of women's silk stockings paralleled the increase in lung cancer also—a coincidence but certainly not causal. Graham later apologized to Dr. Oschner for his silk stocking remark. The apology related to the illness of Dr. Graham, the smoker, who shortly thereafter died of lung cancer.

Ochsner wrote a number of medical articles during the 1930s and 1940s associating lung cancer with smoking. While there were other pioneers who related smoking to lung cancer, Dr. Alton Ochsner was particularly believable because of his stature as an extraordinarily gifted surgeon. He was particularly powerful in linking lung cancer to smoking because, as a chest surgeon, he saw the effects of smoking on the lungs close up and first hand. The initial report on smoking and health of the Surgeon General of the United States was in 1964, a quarter of a century *after* Dr. Ochsner's clinical studies and 10 years after Ochsner's 1954 book, *Smoking and Cancer: A Doctor's Report*.

Not a bad career for a boy born in a sod house on the prairie.

of the great medical cost of smoking, which should be borne by smokers; recall that failure to collect appropriate tobacco taxes are a **subsidy** to the smoker and to the tobacco industry. Nonsmokers have a right to ask why they must support an unhealthy habit and a wealthy industry.

Many people become billboards for their clothing with the out-side tags and maker's logos. Brand loyalty is real for clothing, and as a former smoker, I know it is also just as real for cigarettes. Smoking manufacturers are also aware of brand loyalty and tailor their efforts to generate loyalty among young people. Dr. Dale Kunkel of the University of Arizona has written that point of sale marketing practices urgently need legislative control. This refers to how cigarettes are promoted and advertised at retail stores, which does indeed promote smoking among young people. Dr. Kunkel noted that in 1969, the U.S. Congress banned all advertising for tobacco on radio and television. More recently, the use of cartoon characters such as Joe Camel was banned as well as all outdoor advertising and sponsorship of events that had significant youth audiences. Our government is moving but the pace is slow.

Minnesota was among the first states with clean indoor air legisla-tion. Many states and foreign countries have followed. Canada, Australia, New Zealand, Norway, Sweden, and Ireland all have laws controlling smoking. Obviously, these laws deter smoking and help in smoking ces-sation. Further, noxious secondhand smoke (at least in the smoke-free areas) is greatly reduced.

Informational posters and television spots regarding wrinkles and premature aging of the skin probably are effective. Wrinkling of skin has been repeatedly observed among heavy smokers. A more ominous feature of skin damage due to tobacco is slower healing after surgery. Will these bits of information decrease smoking? Probably not by them-selves but if they become widely known, it may enhance other smoking cessation programs.

Finally, a word about your friendly doctor. A three minute discus-sion of the hazards of smoking at your physical examination seems to be about as effective as drugs, focus groups, television ads, etc. The etymology (relating to the origin of a word) of doctor is "teacher." It is hoped that smokers who read this chapter will get that three-minute teaching lecture. Listen and heed the advice of someone who knows the horror of disease.

SUMMARY

Smoking causes not only lung cancer but also cardiovascular diseases and other forms of cancer. There is no difference in health risk between smoking light cigarettes or regular cigarettes. Because nicotine is addictive, quitting smoking is very difficult, but there are treatments, including drugs and therapy, available to help. Society can take steps and implement laws and programs to discourage people from starting or continuing smoking and to help those who wish to kick the habit.

3

Skin Cancer—Do Not Risk It!

KEY POINTS

♦ Much skin cancer is prevented by reducing exposure to ultraviolet radiation from the sun, tanning beds, and other forms of ultraviolet (UV) light. Avoiding the midday sun and applying sunscreen are other ways to reduce your exposure to UV light.

♦ There are three forms of skin cancer: basal cell carcinoma, squamous cell carcinoma, and malignant melanoma. Basal cell carcinoma accounts for 3 out of every 4 cases of skin cancer. Malignant melanoma is the most lethal of the three.

♦ Check your body at least once a month for irregular spots. When caught early, skin cancer is completely curable.

I was privileged to be selected for officer training at the University of Notre Dame during World War II. For a boy like me, who grew up in the Missouri Ozarks, Notre Dame was a big deal! The campus, even in wartime, was beautiful and I think that most of us navy trainees considered it a wonderful opportunity to study and learn. We were indeed appreciative for this opportunity. The reason for bringing this up is that Notre Dame had an elegant facility called the Rockne Memorial located at the end of a huge quadrangle. The Rockne had a fantastic swimming pool where swimming coach Gil Burdock taught me how to swim—and not far from that pool was a **solarium**. The solarium had a large **ultraviolet** lamp and after a swim, we trainees if we wished could take a "sun bath" in that warm and bright room. It was so soothing and gave us what we thought was a "healthy" tan.

I am an old man now. Old people often have skin problems, and many, including me, have had skin cancer. I sometimes wonder if the assorted spots and blemishes that I carry around as an old man may be due, in part, to that wonderful solarium. Both before and after my Notre Dame experience, I swam for recreation and often, worked out of doors without sun protection. Far be it from me to blame the University of Notre Dame for skin changes that occurred due to my repeated sun exposure since that time more than 60 years ago. I describe the experience to illustrate that few people now and even fewer people then knew of the hazards of exposure to ultraviolet light and to the Sun. Much is now known about how to protect against skin damage, aging, and skin cancer. You will learn about that in this chapter.

A NOTE FOR DARK COMPLEXIONED PEOPLE

This chapter is focused on preventing cancer in the most vulnerable population: people of light complexion. Readers of a darker hue should read the chapter nevertheless—you are extraordinarily fortunate to be at a notably lower risk for skin cancer; but the risk is not zero. Further,

malignant melanoma in people with dark skin is often diagnosed at a later stage than in people with light skin. Late diagnosis of melanoma leads to a cancer that is much more deadly.

HOW COMMON IS SKIN CANCER?

The occurrence of considerably more than 1 million skin cancers per year make skin cancer the most common cancer in the United States. That is the quick answer. While the death rate for skin cancer is low, nevertheless 10,850 people, mostly men, are predicted to die in 2007 (American Cancer Society, Inc. data)—almost all needlessly. Most of the victims who die of skin cancer will die of malignant melanoma. Perhaps a shocking bit of information is that in the United States, the probability of developing invasive (not superficial) malignant melanoma in women from birth to age 39 is second only to that of breast cancer. It follows that the probability for developing invasive malignant melanoma exceeds the probability for developing leukemia, lung cancer, cancer of the uterine cervix, and **non-Hodgkin lymphoma** during those years.

The prevalence of skin cancer increased by 300 percent from 1973 to 2001, and it is still increasing. This chapter will tell you how to avoid skin cancer and be a part of an enlightened group who may yet turn the tide and finally decrease this deadly cancer.

WHO GETS SKIN CANCER?

We are all equal under the law but we are *not* all equal in our vulnerability to specific cancers. White people with fair complexions who freckle and burn easily are far more likely to get skin cancer than their African American friends—or their friends from India. Pigmentation is protective. This is true not only in the United States but also worldwide. Male citizens of Mumbai, India, are 100 times less likely to have skin cancer than white male citizens of Australia and New Zealand. Blonde and red-haired, white citizens with blue eyes are more vulnerable than their dark-haired, dark-eyed fellow citizens; people of Scandinavian or Celtic origin are more likely to develop skin cancer than people of Mediterranean origin.

Of course, lightly pigmented skin does not *cause* skin cancer. As suggested in the introductory paragraphs of this chapter, exposure to ultraviolet radiation causes skin cancer. It makes no difference if the ultraviolet radiation comes from a lamp in a solarium, a lamp in a tanning bed, or from the sun at the seaside—it is the ultraviolet radiation that damages the skin and causes skin cancer. People who are exposed to ultraviolet radiation are the population at risk. Some exposure is on purpose. Note the number of people who sun themselves at the beach to get their desired skin color. But perhaps of greater concern are babies and small children, often of blonde hair with blue eyes, frolicking in the sun while being watched by careless or ignorant parents—the young ones have not chosen to be unprotected and some of them will pay a high price for their exposure.

VARIOUS FORMS OF SKIN CANCER

Automobiles come in diverse models, colors, horsepower, etc. Most people do not become perturbed or confused when they read of a 2005 6-cylinder, 4-door, Buick LaCrosse CXL sedan and they distinguish that car with ease from a 2002 4-cylinder, 4-door Ford Focus SE station-wagon. All cars are not alike and accordingly they have different names and designations. As cars differ, so too do skin cancers. Three kinds of skin cancer will be described briefly—they differ from each other in significant ways—including lethality.

Basal Cell Carcinoma

The most common cancer in the United States is basal cell **carcinoma**. More than 3 of every 4 skin cancers are basal cell carcinomas. Since there are more than a million cases of skin cancer in the United States each year, that makes for a huge number of basal cell carcinomas.

A bit of terminology is in order. The descriptive "basal cell" refers to the deep (basal) layer of **epithelial** skin cells and it is these cells, which have become malignant. Carcinoma is a cancer of epithelial cells. Thus, the term "basal cell carcinoma" tells the knowledgeable reader exactly what kind of skin cancer is under discussion.

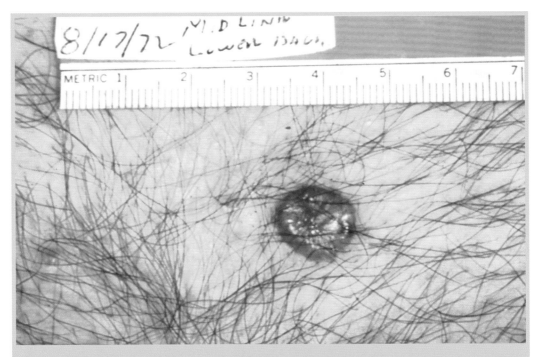

Figure 3.1 Basal cell carcinoma is the most common form of skin cancer in the United States. *(National Cancer Institute/U.S. National Institutes of Health)*

The cure rate for basal cell carcinoma is probably 95 percent or even higher. The high cure rate is a result of the cancer's slow growth and slowness of spreading (metastasis), which gives a good opportunity for removal by a skin doctor. The excellent cure rate also relates to the fact that most people do not want an ugly skin growth. They see skin cancer and when doing so, most seek its removal. An extremely ugly form of this cancer known as "rodent ulcer," which occurs if the basal cell carcinoma is not eliminated in a timely manner. The rodent ulcer has the potential to destroy a large part of the face including an eye and all or part of the nose and/or an ear resulting in horrible and permanent disfigurement. The message here is do not ignore a skin growth.

Squamous Cell Carcinoma

About a fifth of skin cancers are squamous cell carcinomas. This form of skin cancer is the second most common cancer in the United States. It derives its name from the outer layer of the skin epithelium plus the term carcinoma. Squamous cells are scale-like cells that ordinarily flake off and are lost. An individual with repeated exposure to ultraviolet radiation is vulnerable. People with transplanted organs who are on **immunosuppressive drugs** have an increased risk for both the cancer and its spread (metastasis).

Sometimes basal cell carcinomas and squamous cell carcinomas are lumped together as "non-melanomas." This is probably due to the fact that both are considerably less lethal than malignant melanoma.

Malignant Melanoma

This form of skin cancer was once thought to be rare. Malignant melanoma is no longer rare and it is increasing. While melanoma is less common than either basal cell or squamous cell carcinomas, it accounts for about 75 to 80 percent of skin cancer **mortality** (deaths).

Melanoma, as the other two skin cancers discussed here, is believed to be caused by exposure to ultraviolet radiation. The adjective "malignant" is indeed appropriate. Pigment cells in the skin are the cells that become malignant. Early detection of a melanoma is absolutely essential for survival. Localized melanoma has a high cure rate. Cures plunge precipitously if metastasis has occurred. It is far better to *prevent* melanoma than to attempt treatment because survival rates of metastatic melanoma are grim.

Prevention efforts for these three kinds of skin cancer have been mostly ineffective. Failure in prevention is obvious because, while the

Figure 3.2 A malignant melanoma of the skin that shows asymmetry, an irregular border, several colors, and a diameter greater than a pencil eraser. Its evolving state cannot be shown in a single photograph. *(National Cancer Institute/ U.S. National Institutes of Health)*

cause is known, skin cancers continue to increase in number. The often lethal malignant melanoma is largely preventable, but it is still increasing in men (but not in women!).

WHAT IS ULTRAVIOLET LIGHT?

Visible light is but one portion of the electromagnetic spectrum. Electromagnetic radiation with wavelengths longer than X rays but shorter than visible light are known as ultraviolet light. Ultraviolet radiation is invisible to humans but some animals are able to see this part of the light spectrum. The Sun is the chief source of ultraviolet radiation.

Of course, ultraviolet light has wavelengths of various lengths. The longer wavelengths (320 to 400 **nanometers**) are known as ultraviolet A (UV-A); the shorter wavelengths (280 to 320 nanometers) are known as ultraviolet B (UV-B). A third wavelength (100 to 280 nanometers) is called ultraviolet C (UV-C), but this radiation is almost entirely absorbed in the ozone layer and doesn't reach the skin. The DNA genetic material of skin cells is damaged by UV-B radiation and it is the damaged DNA that leads to skin cancer. While tanning lamps are designed to emit primarily UV-A, users of these lamps should be aware that UV-A damages skin elasticity and probably leads to cataract formation. Further, many UV-A lamps inadvertently produce UV-B. The message here is beware!

PREVENTION

Avoid excessive exposure to ultraviolet radiation. Exposure to all forms of ultraviolet radiation, whether from the Sun or manmade, causes skin cancer. All forms include exposure to tanning beds in fitness centers and in tanning salons. It includes sunlamps that can be used in the privacy of the home. Ultraviolet is ultraviolet.

The notion that tanned skin is healthy skin is simply not true. Many people use tanning beds in spite of the known hazards. The obvious reason is that they want their skin to appear more attractive, at least for the present. Beauty is a culturally derived value. It was not long ago when the fair skin of a blonde or redhead was prized as beautiful. Seeking to be attractive is neither evil nor a trivial desire. However, beauty is transient and exposure to ultraviolet radiation hastens wrinkles and a loss of natural elasticity. Ultraviolet radiation accounts for the leathery skin of the habitual sun worshiper, and it causes the brown "age spots" of many elderly people, which are *not* due to aging but result from radiation damage.

WHAT TO WEAR

To retain a youthful skin later in life, avoid unnecessary exposure to the Sun and artificial ultraviolet radiation. Wear protective clothing. A hat with a broad brim that shades the eyes, ears, and face will protect. Baseball hats worn either frontward or backwards do *not* protect the ears. As a result, skin cancer of the ears is becoming increasingly prevalent. Wear dark, densely woven clothing when sun exposure is expected. A quick measure of protection is how much of a shadow a piece of clothing makes. If the shadow is not dark, obviously sunlight, including ultraviolet radiation, is going through the fabric and the fabric provides little protection. Even with protective clothing, reflected ultraviolet light from snow or water can add to the burning effect of the harmful rays. Do not forget eye protection and wear sunglasses that are known to protect against ultraviolet radiation.

Babies should be protected from sun exposure at all times. Young children, who enjoy frolicking in the sun, should be provided with protective hats that shade the face and ears as well as long-sleeved shirts and trousers. It is believed that childhood sunburns are related to adult skin cancer of all types including malignant melanoma.

Time of day matters. Especially important is to avoid the summer sun between 10 A.M. and 4 P.M. The summer sun's rays are far more powerful at noon than in early morning or late afternoon. Do not forget that a cloudy sky filters out only a small amount of ultraviolet radiation; a bad burn can be the result of exposure on an overcast day.

Figure 3.3   A grandmother applies sunscreen to her grandson before spending time outdoors. Both are also wearing protective clothing to avoid excessive sun exposure. *(National Cancer Institute/U.S. National Institutes of Health)*

SUNSCREEN LOTIONS

Avoidance of ultraviolet radiation is the best way to prevent skin cancer. However, every drugstore has a shelf of sunscreen preparations, which many people think protect from the harmful effects of the sun. Sunscreens come in a variety of levels of protection. All provide some protection from ultraviolet B and some protect from ultraviolet A. A higher sun protection factor (SPF) provides greater protection from ultraviolet B but indicates nothing about protection from ultraviolet A. It is wise to find and use sunscreens that protects from *both* ultraviolet A and B. Even with the best sunscreen, protection is never absolute. An SPF of 15 indicates that when the preparation is applied *correctly*, the user can be exposed to burning sun 15 times longer than without the protection. An ample amount of sunscreen must be applied—about one ounce is adequate to protect arms, legs, neck, and face for an adult. Read the label and reapply as directed. Sweating and swimming diminish the protection of most sunscreens and thus special waterproof or water resistant sunscreens should be sought for these special conditions. Apply well in advance before sun exposure. Most products must be absorbed into the skin and this takes up to a half hour. A check of the date on the bottle is necessary because many sunscreens lose their potency with storage or with heat. If the sunscreen package "use by" date has expired, your vulnerability is probably double: One because perhaps you use too little (which is why you still have the unfinished bottle) and two because of reduced protection potential of the aged sunscreen itself.

Any user of sunscreen who is on a prescription drug may be particularly liable to sun damage. If you regularly take medication you have a responsibility to check with your doctor or druggist to find out if the drug you use increases your vulnerability to sun damage.

Even when applied properly, sunscreens provide less than total protection against UV. Sunscreens support the illusion that the user is fully protected. Prolonged exposure to ultraviolet light may be sought because of this illusion. Light complexioned people are most vulnerable to sun damage and it is these who are most likely to use sunscreen. Dark complexioned individuals with dark brown eyes are less likely to use sunscreen than blue eyed blondes or redheads. As a result, many of those who are most vulnerable to ultraviolet damage are exposed for prolonged periods with the notion that they will not fall victim to premature skin aging and skin cancer. They hold this notion at their own peril.

EXCESSIVE EXPOSURE

The term exposure was coupled with "excessive" several times in the preceding paragraphs. Vitamin D is the reason for this. Vitamin D is believed to be related to reduced vulnerability to several cancers including colon cancer, breast, ovarian, and prostate. Generally diet does *not* provide adequate vitamin D. The radiation of the sun augments the level of vitamin D in the body. The correct balance of sun exposure to minimize melanoma hazard and maximize colon cancer prevention is unfortunately unknown. Even the scientists who study cancer thought to be related to inadequate vitamin D agree that exposure to summer sun is hazardous and that protective clothing and sunscreen should be used. A way around this dilemma is to increase vitamin D by oral supplements. Even with this, the optimal amount of vitamin D supplementation is unknown. It is best to remember that "excessive" exposure to ultraviolet radiation is a known hazard for skin cancer. It is wise to keep an eye on vitamin D in the diet. I will not recommend how much vitamin D, but I am confident that the recommended level of the vitamin will likely be increased by our government soon to offset the reduced exposure to sun as recommended by dermatologists.

HOW DO I KNOW IF I HAVE SKIN CANCER?

This chapter is about how to *prevent* skin cancer. Prevention is the name of the game for cancer in this book, but when primary prevention fails for whatever reason, there is another form of prevention. The second form relates to prevention of death by early detection and treatment of a cancer.

It is my belief that diagnosis is the business of the doctor. So, why intrude on the doctor's business? For starters, you see yourself every day; your doctor may see you only once or twice a year. Self-examination for skin cancer in general and melanoma in particular costs nothing. Your self-examination can become an early warning system to help your doctor. In keeping with my stated belief, you may detect a change in a "spot," call it to the attention of your doctor, but your doctor makes the diagnosis. In the end, your self-examination may be a lifesaver. You should not be embarrassed if your doctor tells you that the spot that concerned you is of no medical consequence; indeed, you should be happy if that is what you learn.

A simple memory aid (otherwise known as a "mnemonic device") is the ABCDE scheme for detecting malignant melanoma (and other skin cancers). All of us carry around common moles and benign pigmented lesions—"spots," in other words. The memory aid is designed to help discriminate between the common benign mole and the less common skin malignancy. The "spot" test will help to identify skin lesions that your doctor should examine, and perhaps biopsy for diagnosis, and perform surgery if required. The ABCDE test is

- **A** – **A**symmetry; lack of similarity in shape of the halves of a spot

- **B** – Irregular **B**order

- **C** – Several **C**olors

- **D**iameter greater than 6 mm (about the diameter of a pencil eraser)

- **E**volving (changing) with respect to diameter, shape, color, surface (bleeding), and onset of itching and/or tenderness

The ABCDE scheme is described further in an article by Abbasi and his colleagues in a 2004 issue of the *Journal of the American Medical Association*. The article has excellent color illustrations of the ABCDEs. More information on self-examination can be found on the Web site of the Skin Cancer Foundation (http://www.skincancer.org). The American Cancer Society has a Web page on Skin Cancer Prevention and Early Detection that can be accessed through Google. Self-detection should be done while standing naked before a full-length mirror with a hand held mirror for seeing your back. This should be done at least monthly. However, detection of a new or growing spot is not a diagnosis of malignancy but it does warrant examination and perhaps biopsy by a skilled doctor. Obviously, consultation with a family doctor or dermatologist will provide appropriate information whether a spot is not significant or if it is pre-cancerous or in fact cancer. Remember, *early* diagnosis of melanoma has the potential of a completely curable cancer; delayed treatment may be lethal.

LEARN FROM HISTORY

Southern ladies about the time of the Civil War were known to wear with inordinate pride broad-brimmed hats, fashionable long dresses, long white gloves, and to carry parasols for style and for comfort in the sun. I wonder if they knew that their fashion statement was protection from the southern sun? To learn of this protection, they had to look no further than the poor white farmers who labored in the hot sun and who had aged, weather-beaten skin to show for their efforts. The white workers were vulnerable to skin cancers. The ladies were vulnerable mostly to boredom.

SUMMARY

Skin cancer is generally caused by "excessive" exposure to ultraviolet B (UV-B) radiation. Because the body requires vitamin D, which is provided by sunlight, it's important to remember that "excessive" is the key word. Skin cancer occurs in three forms: basal cell carcinoma, squamous cell carcinoma, and malignant melanoma. Basal cell carcinoma is the most common, but malignant melanoma is potentially deadly. However, most skin cancer is preventable through carefully guarding against exposure to the sun and avoiding artificial sources of ultraviolet radiation.

4

CERVICAL CANCER—PREVENTABLE?

KEY POINTS

◆ Each year, there are about 11,000 new cases of cervical cancer in the United States and approximately 500,000 worldwide. Of that, about 3,700 in the United States and a quarter of a million women worldwide die from cervical cancer each year.

◆ The human papillomavirus (HPV) causes cervical cancer. Most women who are sexually active with several partners have (or have had) an HPV infection. It is caught through intimate contact.

◆ Researchers have introduced a vaccine that produces immunity to HPV infections and thus prevents cervical cancer.

Cervical cancer is one kind of cancer of the uterus. The uterus, also known as the womb, is a pear shaped hollow organ in which a fetus develops during pregnancy. The lining of the uterus is the source of blood and other material lost during the monthly period (**menstruation**). The upper portion of the uterus is known as the **corpus** and the lower portion that extends into the vagina is known as the **cervix**, which is another name for neck. A malignancy that occurs in the neck of the uterus is thus known as cervical cancer.

CERVICAL CANCER IN THE UNITED STATES

An estimated 11,150 new cases of cervical cancer are expected in the United States in 2007. The death toll is predicted to be about 3,670. Virtually all of these cancers are *preventable*. Cervical cancer is rare among young people, but young people should not be indifferent to what it is and how it spreads. Inattention to this now may bring woe later.

CERVICAL CANCER WORLDWIDE

About a half million new cases and a quarter of a million deaths from cervical cancer occur worldwide each year. Mexico leads the world in cervical cancer deaths with a rate more than 500 percent greater than that of the United States. Close to Mexico in cervical cancer death rates are Colombia and Venezuela. As in the United States, the vast majority of these deaths are preventable. Finland is notable because it has the lowest cervical cancer death rate in the world.

Cervical cancer is of great interest for two reasons. The first concern is what causes the cancer (doctors refer to causation as **etiology**). The second relates to the development of a **vaccine** that may protect from this deadly disease. Both of these reasons are important to the readers of this book.

ETIOLOGY

To understand cervical cancer etiology, one must consider who is vulnerable and under what circumstances cervical cancer occurs; that is, one needs to know something of cervical cancer epidemiology. Particularly vulnerable are girls and women who had sexual intercourse early in life, who have had many sexual partners, and whose sexual partners in turn have had many sexual partners. Women who smoke, who have a poor diet, or who have other sexually transmitted diseases are similarly thought to be at increased risk. In contrast, cervical cancer is rare in women younger than 20, among women who abstain from sex (such as nuns with their **celibate** life) and women who have had but one sexual partner who, in turn, had but one sexual partner. This pattern suggests that cervical cancer is a sexually transmitted disease (**STD**). A more precise term is "sexually transmitted infection" (STI) because the disease is not transmitted; rather, an infectious agent is transmitted. The infectious "agent" that is transmitted is a virus.

The virus that gives rise to cervical carcinoma is the human **papillomavirus**. Most women who are sexually active with several partners have (or have had) an HPV infection. It is the most common venereal (sexual) infection among college women in the United States. There is no cure for the viral infection and frequently there are no symptoms. While many women have had the infection, fortunately relatively few will develop cervical cancer.

Human papillomaviruses come in an amazing variety. About 200 kinds are known. Fortunately, not all cause cervical cancer. The best-known, cancer-associated human papillomaviruses are HPV-16 and HPV-18, which are thought to cause about 70 percent of cervical cancer, but others are also known to be associated with cancer.

Transmission of the noxious, cancer-causing HPV is by intimate genital contact. Intimate in this case means skin to skin, and actual sexual intercourse is *not* necessary. The genital contact may be between same sex couples or of different sex couples. Condoms are of limited value in that they do not cover all of the skin adjacent to the penis and thus, skin-to-skin contact is possible, which may lead to HPV infection. However, many health experts still recommend the use of condoms because they reduce the risk for other sex diseases and may possibly also reduce the risk of HPV infection.

HPV as a cause of cervical cancer is a surprisingly useful discovery. Why? To begin with, knowing what causes the cancer provides a way of preventing the cancer. Prevention is simple. Avoid behavior that exposes one to infection by HPV. Cervical cancer, certainly for the most part, is a venereal disease. Avoid any sexual behavior that could lead to a venereal infection. Avoidance of sexual contact has the happy added feature of protection from many other STDs—or as more appropriately suggested above—STIs. It is unfortunate that while prevention through abstinence from promiscuity is easy to understand, it seems to require Herculean effort on the part of many people, and that effort to avoid promiscuous sex seems often to be imperfect. As a result, the HPV is the most common sex disease among young people in the United States.

DETECTING HPV

The primary method for detecting an HPV infection and hence, vulnerability to cervical cancer, is with a **Pap smear**. The term Pap smear is derived from the name of George Papanicolaou, the doctor who developed this method of examination. Cells from the cervical portion of the uterus are taken painlessly by swab and transferred to a slide where the cells are stained and examined with a clinical microscope. The person examining the cells sees exactly that: cells. Viruses are too small to be detected with a clinical microscope. However, a trained **cytologist** (the person who examines the cells) can recognize abnormal cells if present. Certain of these cells indicate that an HPV infection is present. When this occurs, there may be no other symptoms and no treatment may be required other than a re-examination in another three to six months. Alternatively, a doctor may seek further examination with a **colposcope**. The examination, known as a **colposcopy** uses a bright light and magnifying lens to detect abnormalities in or on the cervix. The doctor may perform a minimally painful biopsy with subsequent removal of infected tissue.

It is not the purpose of this book to describe treatment for cancer. This is because, with proper medical attention, no cervical cancer should ever develop. How to prevent infection is known: Do not engage in activity that presents a risk for a sexually transmitted infection. If this warning fails and a HPV infection occurs (as it does in the majority of college women in America), then proper medical care can detect the infection and abnormal cells can be removed. Note: The abnormal cells are removed *before* they have a chance to become cancer. This is prevention at its best.

A VACCINE TO PREVENT CANCER!

Knowing that a virus causes cervical cancer provided researchers with the opportunity to develop a vaccine. The vaccine available in the United States is known as Gardasil and the U.S. Food and Drug Administration approved it for use on June 8, 2006. If, as stated above, death by cervical cancer is preventable, why bother with a vaccine? While modern

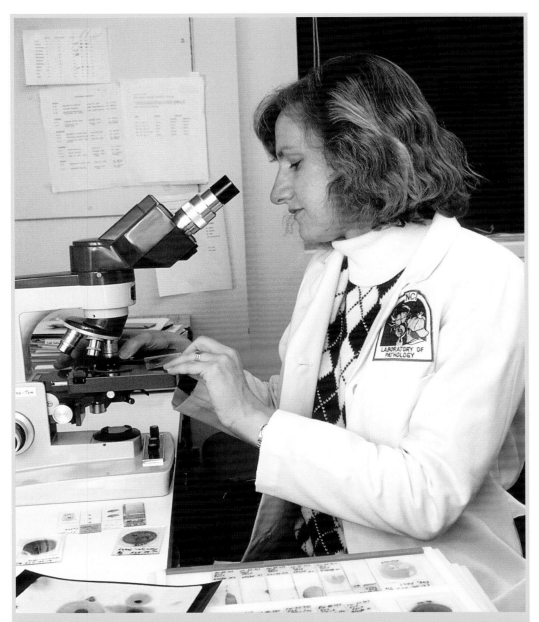

Figure 4.1 Cervical cells in a Pap smear are examined by a cytologist using a compound (clinical) microscope. (*Bill Branson/National Cancer Institute/U.S. National Institutes of Health*)

medical care is available in the United States, inattention to appropriate prevention measures is far too common. Because of inattention, about 11,150 new cases of cervical cancer with 3,670 deaths are expected in 2007 (American Cancer Society, Inc., data). That death rate in the United States is small indeed compared with the lethality of cervical cancer in developing countries worldwide. Clearly, there was a need for a vaccine and it is now approved for use.

Researchers who developed the vaccine are now conducting studies of who should be vaccinated and when that vaccination should take place. The drug is licensed for females age nine to 27. Should young teenagers be vaccinated against HPV? Early vaccination is crucial because the vaccine protects against future infection; it does not cure existing infections. The vaccine should be administered prior to the onset of sexual activity. Thus, the answer to the rhetorical question of whether young persons should be vaccinated is "yes." Some parents strongly object to this, believing that immunity to HPV will encourage earlier sex with an increased number of sexual partners. Other parents consider protection against HPV infection to be a worthy goal and protection against a cancer-causing infection overrides the fear of greater promiscuity. Then there is the question of gender. It may seem nonsensical to vaccinate boys or young men against HPV infection—boys do not get cervical cancer! Of course not, but where do girls get HPV infections? The answer to that question is from boys. If young males do not have an HPV infection, there is no way that they can spread the virus. Vaccination of boys has the potential to reduce HPV infection, and ultimately, reduce cervical cancer.

Gardasil protects against cervical cancer caused by HPV-16 and HPV-18 and what is especially valuable, it also protects against HPV-6 and HPF-11. The latter two HPVs cause genital warts. Genital warts, while

Figure 4.2   A 17-year-old woman gets a shot of Gardasil, the vaccine against human papilloma virus and cervical cancer. (© AP Images)

not malignant are multiple, small, ugly growths that have been described as "cauliflower-like" lesions that can occur in both males and females in the genital area. Genital warts may also occur in the mouth and throat of people who have oral sex with a person with an HPV-6 or HPV-11 infection—such infections are becoming much more common.

Perhaps protection from HPV-6 and HPV-11 in the American vaccine will encourage parents to permit boys to be vaccinated—most parents would not wish a case of venereal warts on their sons and daughters.

♦ A DISCOVERY OF "EXCEPTIONAL IMPORTANCE"

Peyton Rous swam against the current. What does that mean? It means that he had the guts to challenge accepted wisdom. He opened new doors in medical research by doing so. The accepted wisdom of his time was that cancer was "spontaneous." Bacteriologists had sought in vain for a cause of cancer. While bacteria were often isolated from cancers, careful study would invariably show that the bacteria had secondarily infected the cancer and therefore, the cancer was "without cause" (or so it was thought at the time). That kind of work led to the generally accepted notion that cancer was truly a spontaneous disease. Viruses had been considered as possible causes. However, viruses were ordinarily associated with acute infections—cancer is a chronic disease for the most part; untreated, it persists until the patient dies. Thus, viral infections could also be lumped with bacterial infections as not responsible for cancer—again, or so it was thought.

A Plymouth Rock chicken with cancer was brought to Rous' laboratory in 1909. A "soup" was made of the cancer by grinding up the tumor. The soup was filtered to remove all intact cells of any kind (chicken, bacterial, or other), and then, this filtered material was injected into other chickens. It caused cancer in those injected chickens. Rous refrained from using the term "virus." Rather, he reported that there was a "tumor agent" in the filtered "cell-free" preparation. He knew it was a virus and he knew his experiment showed that a virus could cause cancer. He concluded in his now famous 1911 scientific report, ". . . the fact of its transmission by means of a cell-free filtrate assumes exceptional importance." This was the first demonstration that a solid cancer (not a leukemia) was caused by a virus.

This discovery may have assumed "exceptional importance" in the mind of Rous, but it did not in the mind of the scientific community. Viruses and bacteria were not considered good candidates for the cause of cancer as explained above. Further, chickens were clearly unfashionable as laboratory animals; mice, rats, and guinea pigs, yes, but chickens, no! Thus the discovery by Peyton Rous of viruses as a cause of cancer was not given the recognition it richly deserved until he received the Nobel Prize in medicine in 1966—over a half century after his study of "exceptional importance." It should be noted that Nobel Prizes are not given posthumously. Peyton Rous was 87 when he received his Nobel Prize. Had he not lived so long, he would never have received this recognition.

After Rous showed that a virus could cause cancer in a chicken, many other animal cancers were similarly shown to be virus related; these included Lucké's frog kidney cancer, Shope's rabbit papilloma, Bittner's mouse mammary cancer, Gross's mouse leukemia, and others. Much later, some human cancers were shown to be related to, or caused by, viruses and an important example of that are the human papillomaviruses (HPVs).

Francis (he did not use his first name) Peyton Rous was born October 5, 1879; he grew up in Baltimore where he attended medical school at Johns Hopkins University. He cut his hand during an autopsy during his student years and became infected with tuberculosis (TB). He went to Texas seeking a rest-cure from TB and lived for a while in Quanah near the Oklahoma border. His many talents were such that he was hired as a cowboy and participated on horseback in roundups of cattle. In later years, he recalled with pleasure his memory of sitting around the campfire with fellow cowboys. Somehow this outside work must have helped cure his TB

(continues)

(continued)

for he returned to Hopkins to finish medical school in 1905. It was not long after he was invited to the Rockefeller Institute for Medical Research (which later became Rockefeller University) where he did his famous work with chicken cancer.

Peyton Rous died February 16, 1970, at the age of 90 of metastatic cancer. He wrote over 300 scientific articles, 60 of which were written after he retired. Perhaps staying busy, as well as his early life as a Texas cowboy, permitted him to live longer—at least long enough to collect the Nobel Prize in medicine.

The sons and daughters who are protected from HPV strains that cause cervical cancer are at the same time protected from the HPV strains that cause venereal warts. The vaccine is truly a double-whammy!

It is at least possible that in the lifetime of all who read this chapter, cervical cancer will disappear. Thanks to continued medical research and good public health measures, the end of cervical cancer may be in sight!

SUMMARY

Human papillomavirus (HPV) types 16 and 18 cause about 70 percent of cervical cancer. The risk factors for becoming infected with HPV and developing cancer are well-known, making cervical cancer one of the most preventable forms of this disease. Yet, cervical cancer still causes many unnecessary deaths in the United States each year and even

♦ THE PAP TEST

The young couple arrived in the United States almost broke and unable to speak English. They got jobs at the Gimbels Department Store in New York City; she sewed buttons on clothing and he sold rugs. Not an auspicious start for either. Things got better. At the end of his career, he was credited with the greatest medical discovery for cancer prevention in modern medicine—she was his loyal coworker throughout all of their married life. But, that is getting ahead of the story.

He was born George Papanicolaou on May 13, 1883, in the village of Kymi on the island of Evia (aka Euboea) very close to mainland Greece. His father was a doctor and a politician. After being mayor of Kymi, the father was elected to the National Assembly of Greece. The family moved to Athens, where George finished high school and studied medicine at the University of Athens. He graduated as a doctor with high honors at age 21. While he greatly loved most academic subjects—he was an "A" student in medical school—he was not excited about medicine as a career. He went to Germany to study biology where he received a Ph.D. from the Zoological Institute of Munich. In time, he became an underwater life biologist on an oceanographic research vessel with Prince Albert of Monaco. Opportunities were limited for research in Greece at the time so he and his young wife came to the United States in 1913.

Life was not particularly rewarding either intellectually or financially working at Gimbels doing buttons and carpets. George jumped at the opportunity for a research position at Cornell University Medical School. Before long, he was doing reproductive studies using guinea pigs. He was

(continues)

(continued)

annoyed at the prospect of killing many guinea pigs in order to find just a few with eggs at the proper age. He reasoned that female guinea pigs might have a reproductive cycle somewhat similar to humans so he started examining cells taken from the guinea pig vagina. Papanicolaou found that he could detect exactly what part of the reproductive cycle the animals were in by cells obtained on a swab of the reproductive tract. He was delighted because this saved the lives of many guinea pigs. One might call his guinea pig study the original Pap test.

Papanicolaou then extended his studies to humans, and he was excited indeed not only to find normal but also premalignant and even cancer cells on slides prepared from the swabs. Intense study with his coworker wife (she was his first human "guinea pig") eventually led to the Pap test as it is known now. The medical term for loose cells that will adhere to a swab or soft brush is "exfoliated." A cytologist examines exfoliated cells from the woman's cervix using a clinical microscope. The test has the potential of detecting premalignant cells or "precursor" cells of cervical cancer. The test identifies who is in need of subsequent examination and treatment *prior* to the time that the abnormal cells become actual cancer. Those who died of cervical cancer were those who were not screened regularly with the Pap test. As a result, cervical cancer death rates plummeted in countries where the Pap test was regularly used. Literally millions of women are alive because of Dr. George Papanicolaou and his coworker wife Mary. Their screening procedure has been justly called the most significant advance in the prevention of cancer in the 20th century.

more around the world. A vaccine against HPV is available, and regular screening through Pap tests can detect precancerous cells early enough to prevent cervical cancer. These methods, combined with proper attention to this disease, may greatly reduce and perhaps even eliminate deaths due to cervical cancer.

5

CHILDHOOD CANCER SURVIVORS: A PARADOX

KEY POINTS

♦ Chemotherapeutic agent(s), or radiation, or a combination of chemotherapeutic agent(s) *and* radiation are responsible for effectively curing some cancers. However, these same therapies may cause second cancer decades later in life.

♦ Despite the risks of chemotherapy and radiation, those with cancer should opt for cancer therapy. The therapy, however risky, is better than any alternative at this time.

♦ Survivors of childhood cancers should reduce the risk of developing a second cancer by avoiding smoking and excessive sun exposure. Survivors should also make sure to get regular checkups.

What a strange world it is in which we live. Modern medicine (in this case "modern" means, for the most part, post-World War II but especially the 1970s and onward) has developed the very remarkable capability of curing many individuals afflicted with cancers. As stated by our government's Centers for Disease Control and Prevention (CDC), the numbers of people alive who ever received a diagnosis of cancer has increased steadily to an amazing 9.8 million in 2001—they are alive because of advances in early detection and treatment. Cancer has become a curable disease for some and a chronic illness for others. This statement applies to cancer in both children and adults. What a boon that is to those who are saved! Words cannot be written that appropriately express the appreciation and gratitude that we owe to the many researchers who have made cancer cures possible. How many are saved? Currently, it is estimated that three of every four who suffer from childhood cancer will become survivors.

Some of the cancers of young people that respond well to therapy with a high rate of cures are: acute lymphoblastic leukemia, **testicular cancer**, **Wilms tumor**, non-Hodgkin lymphoma, and **Hodgkin's disease**.

So, what is strange about this world? It is the paradox of the contradictory properties of cancer therapy. **Chemotherapeutic agent**, or radiation, or a combination of chemotherapeutic agent *and* radiation have the very real potential of converting a cancer patient into a survivor. That potential has already translated into more than a quarter million young cancer survivors in the United States. However, with survivorship there is risk. The risk is for the development of a second cancer unrelated to the first. The appearance of the second cancer in many, if not most cases, is due to the effects of the successful treatment. The second cancer is a long-term complication of treatment. Because the chemical

Figure 5.1   Children receiving chemotherapy for acute lymphatic leukemia. The child on the left is receiving chemotherapy into her neck and the other child is receiving her chemotherapy into her arm. *(Bill Branson/National Cancer Institute/U.S. National Institutes of Health)*

agents and radiation used to kill cancer cells also affect healthy cells, the agents and procedures that cure also have the potential for causing cancer. That is the paradox.

Is the vulnerability to a second cancer limited to young people? Of course not. Older people are similarly vulnerable. However, it may take several decades for cancer to occur after exposure to a cancer-causing event. There is not much remaining time for a cancer to appear when an 80-year-old person is cured of cancer. Contrast that narrow "window of opportunity" to the years of life that a teenaged survivor expects. Because of the much greater life expectancy of the young person, there is a long window of opportunity for a second unrelated cancer. Hence, there is concern for the survivors of childhood cancer.

In this chapter will be listed specific second cancers and their relationship to chemotherapy and radiation. Here are my views on the paradox. In facing a potential life-threatening cancer in me or a loved one, I know that I would opt for the most effective treatment available as recommended by my doctor. While I have spent a lifetime in the study of cancer, I have neither studied the clinical aspects of cancer nor do I have experience with response to treatment. Thus, I will assume whatever risk that goes with the treatment in the hope that I, or my loved one, might become a survivor. To me, the possibility of becoming a survivor is far preferable than becoming an occupant of a grave. The development of second cancers attributed to therapy is due only to the *success* of that initial therapy—there are no secondary cancers with therapeutic failure. To repeat, second cancers are a complication of *successful therapy*; they do not result from poor medical management. This message translates into the following: Do not forgo lifesaving therapy because of the fear of a *possible* second cancer. Nothing in this chapter is written to suggest one should decline or delay proper treatment of cancer.

NOT ALL SECOND CANCERS ARE DUE TO THERAPY

Second cancers are those that are not related to the first cancer. First cancers, as all cancers, will metastasize in time. The metastatic colonies of cancer are located at anatomically distant sites from the first cancer— the metastases are colonies of the first and are not considered "second" cancers. The metastases are comprised of cells that are identical with the first cancer. Prostate cancer that is metastatic to bone is not bone cancer; it is prostate cancer that has colonized bone. Second cancers are different in every way from the primary cancer.

The term **iatrogenic** means caused by medical treatment. Are all second cancers iatrogenic? The quick answer to that question is "no." Consider life expectancy in the new millennium. It is longer now than ever before. Cancer frequency increases with age. With long life, there are more years for a totally separate cancer to develop for quite different reasons than the first. For example, a childhood survivor of a leukemia may take up smoking in his or her 20s; clearly lung cancer, should it occur in later years, can *not* be attributed to the medicine and procedures of the physician who brought about the cure of the first cancer. Tobacco, not the physician, is the culprit. Other cancers occur for reasons not yet understood and a second cancer may occur purely as a chance event. Some individuals have a genetic susceptibility for multiple cancers, and those multiple cancers would likely occur regardless of treatment. However, many second cancers are due to therapy and some will be discussed, along with what is known about preventing the noxious effects of second cancers.

SPECIFIC CAUSES OF SECOND CANCERS

There are several causes of second cancers among survivors of an initial cancer. These include:

Genetic Predisposition

While **retinoblastoma** is relatively rare it is nevertheless the most common eye cancer of children. There is no known strategy for the prevention of the hereditary form of retinoblastoma. Hereditary means that the disease is a genetically-inherited trait passed down from one's parents and may develop regardless of external cancer factors. The present book is about prevention. Why then is retinoblastoma discussed? It is considered here as an example because about half of the children with the hereditary form of the eye cancer will develop another cancer not related to the retinoblastoma. This ratio compares with perhaps one in 20 children who develop a second unrelated malignancy who have the nonhereditary (or non-inherited type of) retinoblastoma. Clearly, there is a genetic predisposition for a second, unrelated cancer in the hereditary form of retinoblastoma and this is not the fault of modern medical treatment.

Chemotherapeutic Drugs

Etoposide, **teniposide**, and VP-16 are drugs that have been used to treat several kinds of cancers. They are derivatives of **podophylotoxin**, which in turn is derived from the underground roots of an herbaceous plant. These plant derivatives are recognized as inducers of leukemia in some individuals who survived their first cancer with successful therapy. Another chemotherapuetic drug is doxorubicin, an antibiotic derived from *Streptomyces peucetius*, with a potency to treat a wide spectrum of cancer types. Unfortunately doxorubicin, like the podophylotoxin derivates, also has the potential to cause leukemia as a second cancer. A whole group of very reactive and potent chemical agents (including **chlorambucil**, **cyclophosphamide**, **busulfan** and others) are chemicals that cause **leukemia**. The platinum complex drug **cisplatin**, perhaps in interaction with other chemotherapeutic agents, also causes leukemia. The list could be continued. This is not to denounce or condemn specific drugs. The point is to make the reader aware that not one but most cancer drugs can cause cancer. Powerful drugs have powerful side effects. Cancer is an awesome disease requiring powerful drugs. It is unfortunate that cancer is a side effect, but remember, the side effect of a second cancer is a potential hazard *only* to those who have *survived* a first very lethal disease.

Emphasis here has been on leukemias as second cancers. Ordinarily, it takes solid cancers longer to develop than leukemia and thus, less is known about solid tumors as second cancers. However, some solid cancers thought to result from prior treatment of primary cancers are bladder cancer, bone sarcoma, and lung cancer. This list is clearly not

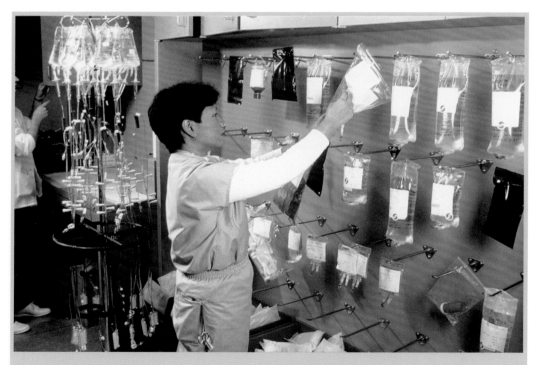

Figure 5.2   Powerful chemotherapeutic agents not only have the potential to cure cancer but may cause, in some cases, a second cancer. Shown here is a health care worker hanging bags of chemotherapeutic agents to be used in the treatment of cancer. *(Bill Branson/National Cancer Institute/U.S. National Institutes of Health)*

exhaustive. The leukemias that occur after successful chemotherapy are mostly **acute myeloid leukemia** (AML) and acute lymphoblastic leukemia (ALL).

Radiation Therapy

X rays were discovered in 1895 by Wilhelm Conrad Roentgen (1845–1923). Roentgen received the Nobel Prize for this discovery because of its immense value in medicine. Workers in the factories that produced X-ray machines used their own hands to test the machines. Primitive X-ray films of the time were slow (insensitive) and thus, the workers' hands received multiple, high doses of X rays—with cancer resulting. The atomic bomb survivors of Hiroshima are known to have an increased prevalence of cancer. Many people fear nuclear reactors. What does all of this tell us? The message is that radiation can cause cancer. It can also cure cancer. Radiation in this regard is not unlike chemotherapeutic drugs—i.e., radiation to cure a first cancer has the potential to cause some second cancers.

Most kinds of cancer can be caused by exposure to ionizing radiation. For example, thyroid cancer is a frequent complication of the treatment of Hodgkin's disease. Other second cancers following therapeutic radiation include cancers of the central nervous system, bone **sarcoma**, and breast cancer. As before, nothing stated here is to suggest that a cancer patient avoid potentially lifesaving therapy.

STRATEGY FOR SURVIVORS OF CANCER

For a successful strategy, those who are at risk must be informed that they are at risk. For whatever reason, a significant number of childhood cancer survivors are *unaware that they are indeed survivors*, perhaps because they were judged too young to understand potential

◆ THE DISCOVERY OF A CHEMOTHERAPY DRUG

It was so cold the water pipes froze and burst. That was the night in 1918 (January 23 to be specific) when Gertrude Belle Elion was born. Fortunately, her mother chose to give birth in a hospital rather than subjecting her newborn to a shower of cold water. Both of Gertrude's parents were immigrants. Her mother was born in a part of Russia that is now Poland; her father was born in Lithuania. During the Great Depression the Elions were less than affluent. Gertrude attended her local high school in the Bronx, in New York City. She won admission to Hunter College, New York City, from whence she graduated in 1937 with high honors in chemistry. Hunter College was a tuition-free college at the time (it is no longer) and Gertrude Elion attended it because, for among other reasons, money was scarce.

Students of today know that grades are the ticket to professional school. Gertrude wanted to get an advanced degree in chemistry. Therefore, as an honors graduate of Hunter, she applied to the chemistry departments of 15 universities. Rejection letters came from all 15. One of the departments wrote: "You're qualified. But we've never had a woman in the laboratory before, and we think you'd be a distracting influence."

Among the jobs she took was that of a substitute teacher in high school chemistry at $7.50 per day. In 1944 she was hired by Burroughs Wellcome, a pharmaceutical company, and she worked for them for the next 39 years. It was her job to study DNA in disease and attempt to find a metabolic "Achilles heel." DNA replicates in cell division and she speculated that if she could interfere with the metabolism of one of the components of DNA (in this case a purine), she might discover a means of blocking cell division.

With persistence, she was able to synthesize **6-mercaptopurine (6-MP)** which did indeed interfere with cell division—to the extent that it became a major component of the treatment of leukemia. For sophisticates of chemistry, please note that Elion's studies were done before the double-helix structure of DNA was known. Despite that fact, she discovered a way to block DNA replication and therefore, cell division. All of the 15 chemistry departments that rejected Gertrude Belle Elion must have been shamed when

Figure 5.3 George Hitchings (left) and Gertrude Elion (right) won the Nobel Peace Prize for designing drugs that could fight pathogens without harming healthy human cells. (© AP Images)

she received a Nobel Prize in medicine in 1988. Regardless of her lack of the Ph.D., she received 23 honorary doctorates.

Gertrude Elion probably was not pleased, nor surprised, to learn that her powerful 6-mercaptopurine is, with probably most other chemotherapeutic agents, implicated in some second cancers. I would speculate, that

(continues)

(continued)

were Elion still alive, she would be at work to develop a gentler chemo-therapeutic agent to use instead of the 6-mercaptopurine. And, knowing how devoted she was to her scientific work, I feel certain she would in time, have been successful. Would that she were still alive! She died February 21, 1999.

complications of their cancer treatment. This is unfair to the survivor. It is unfair because the survivor must marshal every available procedure to minimize the chances or severity of a second cancer. As most would say, "one is enough." It is said that lightning never strikes the same place twice, but the young survivor must realize that is not true in the case of cancer. Being aware will protect to a very real extent; properly managed awareness clearly reduces risk.

The survivor must become knowledgeable about established and newly developed screening procedures so that he or she may work in close collaboration with his or her doctor for early detection of a second cancer should one occur. Screening for cancer should *not* be viewed as a morbid preoccupation. There should be a significant degree of happiness each time a screening procedure reveals no new cancer. And, if there is an unfortunate second cancer, the survivor will know it was detected early for the best treatment.

Smoking avoidance should be a personal high priority for survivors. Of even greater importance is smoking cessation, if the survivor has taken on this habit. Survivors must not use tobacco in any form. Further, the survivor must avoid secondhand smoke. Smoking cessation is discussed in Chapter 2. Other prevention strategies include attention to a proper diet and exercise (see Chapter 7) and protection from the sun (see Chapter 3). Regular physical checkups are essential as a part of the screening procedures described in the preceding paragraph.

HONOR THE DOCTORS WHO SAVED YOUR LIFE

Survivors of cancer may become apprehensive about a second cancer and develop an antagonism for the medical team that saved his or her life after reading this chapter. Do not become angry. Cherish your life and give your doctors the appreciation that they deserve. You are at an increased risk for a second cancer and that cannot be denied. But there are well known ways of minimizing risk for that cancer and they are described above. Give prevention your best effort and strive to make something useful and beautiful of your life. Only a few short years ago, your life would not have been spared. Knowledge of your new life expectations should be a message for personal achievement—keep your doctors informed on how well you are doing. They will appreciate hearing from you.

SUMMARY

Using chemotherapy and radiation treatments, doctors can cure many types of cancer, but these treatments, which affect healthy cells as well as cancerous cells, bear the risk of inducing second cancers later in the patient's life. For this reason, anyone who has been successfully treated for cancer must be extremely vigilant in taking preventive measures and following proper screening practices to protect against the development of a new cancer.

6

BREAST CANCER—PREVENTABLE?

KEY POINTS

♦ Breast cancer in women is second only to lung cancer as a cause of death by malignancy in the United States.

♦ Women who had their first child under age 18 had only a third to 40 percent of the breast cancer of women who delayed having a child until after age 35. Any delay in age at pregnancy and first birth will slightly increase breast cancer risk, including having no children at all.

♦ Other risks of breast cancer include genetic mutations such as those to the BRCA1 and BRCA2 genes, obesity, family history, race, and age of first menstruation.

♦ Risk reduction includes moderating consumption of alcohol, exercise, and breast-feeding for at least one year after giving birth.

Bernardino Ramazzini (1633–1714) was born in the northern Italian town of Carpi. He received a doctor of philosophy and medicine degree in 1659 from the ancient and distinguished University of Parma. At some time in his career he became interested in the relationship between how people made a living and the diseases from which they die. He is mentioned at the beginning of this chapter because he observed that nuns in Italy of that time had more breast cancer than women who were not nuns. The breast cancer was caused, Ramazzini wrote, "in my opinion, by their celibate life . . . every city in Italy has several religious communities of nuns, and you seldom can find a convent that does not harbor this accursed pest, cancer, within its walls." His book on occupational cancer, *De Morbis Artificium*, which included the nun story, was published in 1700.

If an occupational group, in this case nuns, are found to have a different prevalence of breast cancer from other women, then one may ask what it is about the occupation that causes the difference. Can understanding what causes the difference be useful in reducing cancer rates in the special group and in the general population who are at a different risk?

Ordinarily, nuns are women who take vows of chastity—in other words, they have a celibate life. Ramazzini believed that it was their celibate life that was causing their breast cancer. Celibacy means doing without sex for religious reasons. Surely, abstaining from sex should not cause cancer. What else is related to celibacy? Among other things, no sex means no children. Nuns forego having children their entire lives. Before proceeding further, perhaps the epidemiological breast cancer data should be updated. After all, Ramazzini published his book in 1700, which makes the nun story a bit dated. Perhaps for clarity, instead of focusing on celibacy it would be informative if we considered the nuns as **nulliparous** (from the Latin *nullus*, meaning "none" and *parere*, meaning "to bear") women, or women who never became pregnant and bore children. Let us now compare not just nuns but other nulliparous women with women who do have children. Fortunately, this has been done. And, it seems that in general, Ramazzini was correct. **Multiparous** (from the Latin *multi*, meaning "many" and *parere*) women have less breast cancer than do women who are nulliparous. Having a large number of children requires starting the pregnancy business early. Because of that fact, investigators decided to study the age of women at the birth of their first child.

THE MOTHER'S AGE AND BIRTH OF HER FIRST CHILD

A study was published in 1970 in the *Bulletin of the World Health Organization* called, "Age at first birth and breast cancer risk," that looked at the age of women at the birth of their first child and their relative risk for breast cancer. The investigators studied women of different geographical sites and ethnic groups; these included women of Boston, Massachusetts; Glamorgan, Wales; Athens, Greece; the Republic of Slovenia; Sao Paulo, Brazil; Taipei, Taiwan; and Tokyo, Japan. They found a striking relationship between their age and incidence of breast cancer. Women who had their first child under age 18 had only a third to 40 percent of the breast cancer compared to women who delayed having a child until after age 35!

This is one kind of epidemiological data that could be exploited for prevention, at least in theory. The theory would suggest a massive decrease in breast cancer prevalence if all women had their first child before age 18. I can hear some college-destined (or medical school, law school, engineering, theological seminary, or you name it) women thinking, "Great! Just exactly how am I to enter college and medical school while caring for one or more small children?" The real message here for prevention is not to have children early; it is to look at epidemiology to seek *practical* clues to cancer prevention. Are there any for breast cancer?

RISK FACTORS

Breast cancer is second only to lung cancer as a cause of death by malignancy in the United States (perhaps this will stimulate a reexamination of the significance of smoking in those women who enjoy tobacco—you smokers, go back and reread Chapter 2). While lung cancer kills more, the toll on women by breast cancer is sufficiently great that preventive measures of this terrible disease must be considered. The American Cancer Society, Inc. estimates that there will be 178,480 new cases and 40,460 deaths of women by breast cancer in the United States in 2007. For comparison, about 16,000 to 17,000 Americans are expected to die of AIDS in 2007.

A risk factor is any condition that increases one's chance of getting a particular disease. Here, we consider breast cancer risk factors. It must be remembered that "chance" is just that: A woman may have a breast cancer with no known risk factors or she may have several risk factors and be disease-free. Risk factors are presented to inform readers about causes of cancer; most cannot be changed but some can.

Risk Factors That Cannot Be Changed

Gender. The reader may think, "Duh, what a no brainer!" Obviously, women have breasts and thus are vulnerable. But, it is not as simple as all that. About 2,030 (less than 1 percent of the female rate) new cases

Diet and lifestyle factors in breast cancer

A third of cancer deaths in the United States are thought to be due to poor diet and lack of exercise, but few direct links have been made between specific foods or types of foods and specific cancers. Diet may play less of a role in hormone-related cancers such as breast and prostate cancer. Studies have found these factors may affect the odds of getting breast cancer:

Weight	Alcohol	Fat	Meat	Fiber	Fruits and vegetables
Being obese or overweight raises risk, especially after meno-pause	More than a drink a day raises risk	Results are inconsistent, but lower breast cancer rates are seen in coun-tries where diets are lower in fat	High consump-tion of red meat and animal fats may raise risk	in high levels may reduce estrogen, which may lower breast cancer risk, but evidence is unclear	reduce risk; at least five servings a day are recom-mended

SOURCES: American Cancer Society; National Cancer Institute   AP

Figure 6.1   © *AP Images*

of breast cancer in males will be diagnosed in 2007 according to the American Cancer Society. Thus, female sex is judged as a significant risk factor but males, at a far lower rate, are also vulnerable.

Age.   Women between 20 and 29 have only a fraction of a percent chance of developing breast cancer. More than three-fourths of breast cancer is diagnosed in women over the age of 50. Of course, a particular woman's risk will be higher or lower depending upon other known and unknown factors.

Age at the Birth of First Child.   For practical reasons, most women in the United States delay having children beyond the age of 18. Any delay in age at pregnancy and birth will slightly increase breast cancer risk including the ultimate delay, having no children at all. This is still true for nuns as it was 300 years ago.

Genetics.   Several specific **mutations** affect breast cancer vulnerability; these include mutations to BRCA1 and BRCA2 (the "BR" stands for breast, "CA" indicates cancer, and the number refers to the particular gene. One of these genes, BRCA1, accounts for about 5 percent of breast cancer. That number translates to 1 in 20, which does not seem like many until it is realized that nearly 41,000 women die of breast cancer in the United States each year. Five percent of the annual toll is more than 2,000, a not inconsiderable number. Mutations to BRCA1 are particularly common in the breast cancers of Ashkenazi women (*Ashkenazim* is a Hebrew word meaning "Germany" and it refers to Jews who lived in the Rhineland valley and nearby areas of France prior to moving to Russia and the Ukraine and then elsewhere). Women who have mutations to *either* BRCA1 or BRCA2 have a lifetime risk for breast cancer of 60 percent to 80 percent. That should be compared with the lifetime risk of women who do not have those mutations of only 12 percent.

Human epidermal growth factor receptor gene 2, better known as HER2, is a gene that is overexpressed in breast cancer. Overexpression of a gene means that the gene is producing too much of its gene product. This occurs in somewhat more than a quarter of all breast cancer patients. Overexpression of HER2 leads to a more aggressive form of breast cancer with rapid cell growth and a high metastatic potential. Women with overexpression of the gene are known as HER2 positive.

Most cancer chemotherapy involves control of cancer growth by killing cells. This is known as cytotoxic chemotherapy and losing hair and nausea are recognized as two of the many toxic side effects. Many people hope that chemotherapy will advance from conventional chemotherapy (which generally fails to distinguish between normal and cancer cells) to a more cancer-cell-specific therapy. This seems to be the case in breast cancer treatment with an **antibody** that targets cancer cells that have overexpression of the HER2 gene. The exact mode of action of the antibody is not yet known but what is known is exciting indeed. The antibody with the proper name of trastuzumab (Herceptin is the trade name) inhibits cancer cell proliferation in HER2 positive women. Other genes are known to be involved in breast cancer growth.

Family History.   My brother has prostate cancer. That fact elevates *my* risk for prostate cancer. I am completely powerless to sever my blood relationship with my brother even if I wanted to (which I do not—at least most of the time). In a somewhat similar fashion, women who have blood relatives, such as daughters, mothers, sisters, referred to as "first-degree relatives," who have had breast cancer are at twice the risk compared to women who do not. Risk is increased further if two or more blood relatives had breast cancer, or if they had both breast and ovarian cancer, or if the cancers occurred prior to the age of 50, or if a male blood relative has breast cancer, or if there are Ashkenazi Jewish relatives. Obviously these risk factors are not subject to change.

Personal History.   A woman who previously had breast cancer is at a significantly higher risk to develop a second breast cancer. The risk is more than three times that of a woman who has not had breast cancer.

Race.   White women have a slightly increased risk compared with African American women. Asian and Native American women have a reduced risk compared with white women.

Menstruation.   Girls who have their first monthly period at an early age (before 12 years of age) are at an increased risk, as are women who are more than 55 years old when they undergo menopause.

Radiation Therapy to the Chest.   Young women who received radiation therapy to the chest for another cancer are at elevated risk for breast cancer. This statement does not pertain to the breast cancer screening technique called **mammography**. Mammography obviously involves radiation. Note that therapeutic radiation involves a *much* greater dose of radiation than does mammography. Ordinarily, young women are *not* given routine mammographic evaluation.

Other Risk Factors.   Because breast cancer has been studied so extensively, it should not come as a surprise that a multitude of other correlates have been described. One example is that previous benign breast disease and/or previous abnormal breast biopsy increases risk (this does *not* include **fibrocystic** breasts). During World War II and for a decade or so thereafter, pregnant women at risk of a spontaneous abortion (miscarriage) were given a drug called diethylstilbestrol (DES) to save their babies. Those now grown babies have a slightly increased risk for breast cancer. Some women at menopause have a variety of symptoms (hot flashes, mood swings, reduced sex drive, etc.) and treatment for these and other menopausal symptoms may involve hormone replacement therapy (HRT). HRT decreases coronary heart disease and **osteoporosis** risk, but when HRT involves both estrogen and progesterone, there is an increased vulnerability to breast cancer.

What You Can Do to Reduce Risk

Consumption of Alcohol.   It is estimated that having several (two to five) drinks a day results in women who have 1.5 times the risk of nondrinkers. This risk factor can be easily controlled by all women other than those who suffer from alcoholism. Accordingly, women who wish to minimize their risk for breast cancer should consider limiting alcohol consumption—if they consume alcohol at all. The term that is important here is alcohol, i.e., ethyl alcohol. Ethyl alcohol in any form: beer, wine, brandy, whisky (bourbon, scotch, Irish or "the white lightning" of the Missouri Ozarks; it makes no difference; all contain much alcohol) taken in excess will increase risk for breast cancer.

Maintenance of a Proper Weight.   Many epidemiological studies have shown that obesity is related to breast cancer but the relationship is controversial. Weight gain after age 18 seems to increase breast cancer that occurs after menopause. Obesity results from an intake of dietary calories in excess of those burned or as a result of inadequate physical activity.

Exercise.   Sedentary women are thought to have an increased risk for breast cancer. An impressive alternative to the sedentary lifestyle is jogging, but walking is easier. How much walking? The Women's Health Initiative, a study of 161,808 women, reported that brisk walking for 1.25 to 2.5 hours a week will reduce breast cancer risk by 18 percent. Walking for 10 hours reduces the risk to an even greater extent. Think of it. No special equipment. No drugs. No expensive athletic attire or "running" shoes. No painful workout. Just walk. Get started now!

One may ask ,"How does exercise affect my breasts?" Good question! It was noted earlier that onset of menstruation at an early age increases breast cancer risk. Young women who participate in vigorous athletic activity have a delay in onset of menstruation and lowered serum estrogen. These are in turn are thought to result in a reduced risk. Exercise also may lead to a leaner body—obesity is a correlate of breast cancer; exercise and lose that body fat!

Breast-feeding.   "The longer women breast-feed the more they are protected against breast cancer. The lack of or short lifetime duration of breast feeding typical of women in developed countries makes a major contribution to the high incidence of breast cancer in these countries."

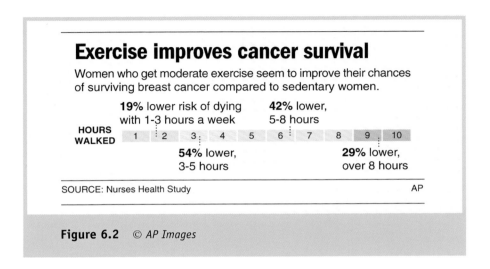

Figure 6.2   © *AP Images*

A rhetorical question: Can the risk for breast cancer be quantified? The answer is "yes" for *group* averages; the answer is "no" if one seeks the exact risk for a particular individual. What are the risk factors with nursing? "The relative risk for breast cancer decreased by 4.3% . . . for every 12 months of breast-feeding in addition to a decrease of 7.0% . . . for each birth." These findings were reported by Beral in 2002 in *The Lancet*. The ellipses indicate deleted statistical material, which makes this data reliable—for those who seek the statistical information, the full citation for this article appears in the Further Resources section. The authors of this monumental (about 147,000 women) study further stated: "These relations are significant and are seen consistently for women from developed and developing countries, of different ages and ethnic origins, and with various childbearing patterns and other personal characteristics."

The reader must bear in mind that the data are *averages of groups*; the data cannot be extended to individuals with any validity. Nevertheless, I cannot help but be reminded of my long-dead mother who had three children and nursed each for one year. A calculation: 3 times 7 percent (21 percent) for bearing each child plus 4.3 percent times 3 (12.9 percent) for nursing each child one year. If these reductions in breast

♦ **WHAT DO CHIMPANZEES AND BREAST CANCER HAVE IN COMMON?**

A first answer to the question posed by the title of this essay is "not much." However, in reality, the cancer and the small primate do have a few things in common. For starters, it should be stated that the DNA (the genome) of the chimpanzee was studied by Professor Mary-Claire King. King also identified the first gene, BRCA1, known to be related to breast cancer. So, the monkey and the cancer have in common that they were studied by the same distinguished scientist. For one person to work on such disparate projects and to make profound and major contributions to *both* is unusual to the extreme.

Mary-Claire King, and her coauthor A.C. Wilson, showed in a study that the genetic material DNA and its products in chimpanzees and humans are nearly identical. Nearly identical here means about 99 percent. The issue here is that subtle DNA differences can result in vast dissimilarities in organisms.

King began a study looking for a single gene that would be related to breast cancer. The gene in its normal form would, among other things, suppress the formation of cancer. Cancer would likely develop if the gene were found in a mutant form. The DNA genetic material of a human is vast indeed—to look for a single gene mutation that would account for cancer was thought to be an endeavor not likely to succeed. But Dr. King and her

cancer are cumulative as the data suggest to some, then that calculates as a whopping 33.9 percent reduced risk for breast cancer—my mother's group average. She would have been pleased to inform readers that, as

colleagues found a single gene difference, which is now known as BRCA1. BRCA1 in its mutant form(s) causes a hereditary form of breast cancer in a small group of women—but in that small group, it has the potential for inducing cancer in the majority of those who have the gene.

King showed that subtle changes in DNA characterize the differences between a monkey and humans; perhaps in a somewhat similar fashion, the mutation of BRCA1, which changes only a tiny fraction of the total genomic DNA, has the potential to alter normal cells and to render them malignant. Minute variations to DNA can pack an immense wallop!

It is now possible to screen for the presence of mutant BRCA1 and thus detect who is at a very high risk for breast cancer. Does this help in the prevention of cancer? No. But the detection of who is at high risk saves lives. And, by knowing more about how mutant genes brings about cell transformation to cancer will enable scientists and doctors to understand the process. Understanding cancer holds the promise of *preventing* cancer.

Mary-Claire King was born February 27, 1946, in Evanston, Illinois. She attended Carleton College in Northfield, Minnesota, and graduated in mathematics *cum laude*. She received her Ph.D. in genetics from the University of California, Berkeley, and she has received many honorary doctorates since that time. She is currently American Cancer Society professor in the departments of medicine (medical genetics) and of genome sciences, University of Washington, Seattle.

many of her group, she did *not* die of breast cancer. My daughters nursed even longer—it is my hope that they too will be spared.

It is my desire that the women readers of this chapter will consider breast feeding of their children yet to be born and join my mother's group in enjoying a reduced risk for breast cancer.

Tamoxifen and Women at High Risk.   Tamoxifen is a drug given to some women to prevent the recurrence of breast cancer. It is not an elective for most women. It is given by prescription only to women at high risk whose breast cancer expresses estrogen and progesterone receptors. Strictly speaking, it does not prevent occurrence of cancer; rather as indicated, its role is to prevent recurrence.

Reduction of risk for breast cancer is possible for many women as discussed in this section. The future may hold even more promise.

WHAT DOES THE FUTURE HOLD?

The answer to the question, "Is breast cancer preventable?" is: "Well, to some extent but not by much." That's not to say there is no hope for a better future. It is worth mentioning here that while breast cancer is certainly and reasonably to be feared, most women do not get breast cancer (7 of every 8 women will *not* get that cancer during their entire life) and *most* of those who do will survive (the lifetime risk of dying from the dreaded malady is 1 in 28). Those statistics are encouraging but we must do better. Of that, there is no choice. Epidemiology is a branch of science that holds the potential of reducing breast cancer prevalence. Mentioned in this chapter is the astonishing conclusion that breast cancer risk could be deeply cut if women breast-fed their children for the length of time that women do (or used to do) in developing countries. That data shows the power of analytical epidemiology. Are there other modes of behavior yet to be discovered that, if exploited by all or most women, would similarly decrease breast cancer? If so, epidemiologists will discover those preventive factors sooner or later. I hope it is sooner. In the meantime, young mothers might well consider breast-feeding as a practical, inexpensive, non-drug procedure for reducing breast cancer risk.

Another kind of research involves genetic analysis. The discovery of specific **mutant** genes that cause breast cancer (or any other cancer for that matter) holds the promise that knowing the variant gene, its product, and how the gene product causes cancer, will permit molecular biologists to devise ways of replacing the mutant gene, or blocking the production of the mutant gene product, or introduction of another gene or its product that will abrogate (block) the effects of the mutant gene. That sounds complex, but all of the procedures requisite for these genetic manipulations are available, waiting to be exploited, and beginning efforts are underway and promising. Now, molecular biology is focused primarily on treatment but in the near future, modes of prevention with these marvelous tools of science will emerge.

SUMMARY

Breast cancer is not readily preventable, but there are many steps women can take to reduce their risk of developing it. These include lifestyle changes, such as keeping fit and getting regular exercise as well as either not drinking alcohol or having no more than one drink per day. Other major factors are pregnancy, childbirth, and breast-feeding; women who have children and have breast-fed them reduce their breast cancer risk significantly. Some breast cancer is hereditary, and specific genes related to breast cancer have been identified. While this doesn't allow the prevention of cancer, it does help in screening and monitoring those women at high risk, so that if cancer develops it can be treated early.

7

Diet and Exercise
Do Make a Difference

KEY POINTS

♦ Many cancer researchers believe that diet is related to perhaps 30 to 40 percent of all cancers. These cancers are believed to be related primarily to high fat, low fiber, and fried food. A healthy diet consists mostly of plant sources and limited consumption of meat.

♦ Even though the link between diet and cancer is controversial, those who follow nutrition guidelines will enjoy better health and put themselves at a lower risk for coronary heart disease and diabetes.

♦ Obesity is a significant threat to life expectancy. Diet and exercise help reduce the threat of obesity.

Several years ago, I received an honorary doctor of science degree from Drury University in Springfield, Missouri. There is a required talk that goes with receiving the degree. I chose to speak about cancer and diet. As I described what I thought were appropriate foods that might reduce risk for that abominable disease, I reflected that the recommended meals were very close to the meals my mother gave me when I was a small boy. I remember well her telling me to eat my greens and other veggies, to eat the whole wheat bread on my plate, and to enjoy the fresh fruit she put out as a dessert. I remarked to the graduating students that nutrition scientists could have saved a lot of research money by just listening to my mother. I suspect that most mothers similarly encourage a good diet for their offspring, a diet that is not only good for growing boys and girls but a diet that is believed by many to be good for helping to prevent cancer. If you hear similar words from your mother, listen to her.

Contrast what my mother advocated with the fast-food fare that many people choose today. A fast-food meal may be made up of sugar water with caramel coloring and some flavoring (a "cola" drink), potatoes deprived of their skin and treated with hot oil (french fries), and cooked fatty hamburger meat served on bleached white flour baked in the form of a soft, bland bun. I wouldn't feed that concoction to a pet dog—or to any other pet—much less a child of my own.

WHAT YOU EAT MAY SAVE YOUR LIFE

Nutrition and food are thought by many cancer researchers to be related to perhaps 30 percent to 40 percent of all cancers. These cancers are believed to be related primarily to consumption of high fat, low fiber, and fried food. The principal cancers related to these dietary factors are cancers of the colon, breast, pancreas, prostate, ovary, kidney, and **endometrium**. Inadequate levels of fruit and veggies are thought by some to be related to stomach and other cancers. I agree with Gary M. Williams and Ernest L. Wynder that "definitive proof of causation is difficult to establish . . . Nevertheless, public health action does not have to await irrefutable evidence of causality." I shall take the view that recommended "cancer preventing" diets could enhance other aspects of good health and just *may* protect against cancer—what is there to lose?

The significance of diet extends beyond simply eating the right foods. It must also include a serious consideration of caloric intake (how *much* one eats) and the amount of physical exercise that one gets. Together, the amount of good food and the extent of physical activity will result in either a proper weight throughout life—or the very real possibility of the pathological effects of obesity. The last paragraph of this chapter addresses the dire consequences of an obese America—if you do nothing else, read and remember that last paragraph.

FIGHT CANCER WITH YOUR KNIFE AND FORK

Wendy Demark-Wahnefried, a professor in the department of surgery at Duke University Medical School, wrote in the magazine, *Coping,* "Fight cancer with your knife and fork by eating plenty of vegetables, fruits and whole grains, and eating less red meat and fatty foods (especially saturated fat from animal sources)." Dr. Demark-Wahnefried's remarks were directed to cancer survivors—her recommendations are just as appropriate to people who wish to *prevent* cancer.

Regarding mega doses of vitamins and antioxidants sometimes consumed to protect against cancer: A balanced diet of vegetables, fruit, cereals, and fat-free dairy products contains everything that an ordinary person needs for good nutrition. Seeking to enhance that good diet

Figure 7.1 Fight cancer by eating plenty of vegetables, fruits, and whole grains, as illustrated here, is the advice of Dr. Demark-Wahnefried. *(National Cancer Institute/U.S. National Institutes of Health)*

by large doses of vitamins and antioxidants is unnecessary, and, if an undetected cancer is present, *might* even enhance the growth of that as yet to be discovered malignancy. Many oncologists discourage cancer patients from using antioxidants during chemotherapy and radiation treatment because the very antioxidants that ordinarily protect normal cells might encourage cancer cells. For any cancer patient who happens to read this, the author urges that patients consult with their oncologist and heed the advice of the person in charge of therapy.

NUTRITION IS NOT
WITHOUT CONTROVERSY

Controversy abounds in the modern world. Many people believe in special creation; others favor evolution. Some citizens wish to build football stadiums; others seek funds for art museums or university cancer centers. Cigar and cigarette smokers want their freedom to light up in restaurants, while others demand clean air and a ban on smoking in eating places. I focus on controversy to make it perfectly clear that there is no unanimous view about the role diet plays in cancer. One needs only to refer to the enormous tome (2,898 pages not including a 300+ page index) of *Cancer, Principles & Practice of Oncology,* 7th edition, edited by V.T. DeVita Jr., S. Hellman, and S.A. Rosenberg, published in 2005 by Lippincott Williams & Wilkins, to find statements such as: ". . . any conclusions should be regarded as tentative" with regard to fat in the diet (on page 511); as to fiber, "observational data presently available do not indicate an important role for dietary fiber in the prevention of cancer" (on page 517); and concerning fruits and veggies (my mother would not like this), "doubts have been cast on the protective association between fruit and vegetable consumption and cancer" (on page 518).

However this may be, my view of nutrition and cancer is in harmony with the American Cancer Society (ACS) Guidelines on Diet and Cancer Prevention, which, incidentally, are essentially identical with the recommendations of the American Institute for Cancer Research (AICR) and are similar to the recommendations of the National Cancer Institute and the American Heart Association. The ACS guidelines for cancer prevention are thought to offer the best nutrition information currently available to the citizens of the United States. They are offered

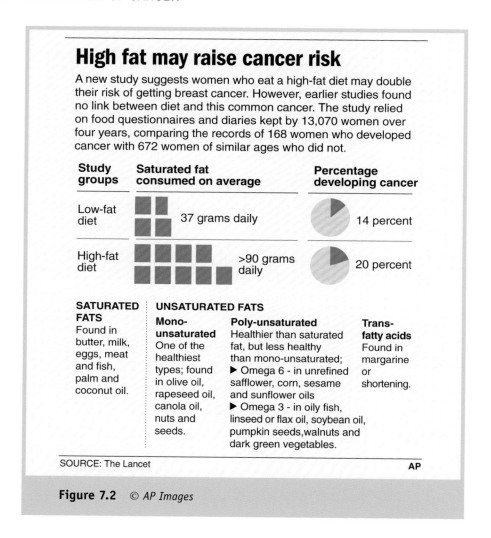

High fat may raise cancer risk

A new study suggests women who eat a high-fat diet may double their risk of getting breast cancer. However, earlier studies found no link between diet and this common cancer. The study relied on food questionnaires and diaries kept by 13,070 women over four years, comparing the records of 168 women who developed cancer with 672 women of similar ages who did not.

Study groups	Saturated fat consumed on average	Percentage developing cancer
Low-fat diet	37 grams daily	14 percent
High-fat diet	>90 grams daily	20 percent

SATURATED FATS
Found in butter, milk, eggs, meat and fish, palm and coconut oil.

UNSATURATED FATS

Mono-unsaturated
One of the healthiest types; found in olive oil, rapeseed oil, canola oil, nuts and seeds.

Poly-unsaturated
Healthier than saturated fat, but less healthy than mono-unsaturated;
▶ Omega 6 - in unrefined safflower, corn, sesame and sunflower oils
▶ Omega 3 - in oily fish, linseed or flax oil, soybean oil, pumpkin seeds, walnuts and dark green vegetables.

Trans-fatty acids
Found in margarine or shortening.

SOURCE: The Lancet   AP

Figure 7.2   © AP Images

in this chapter with the thought that the readers who abide by the recommendations may profit from a reduced risk for cancer. Even if this ultimately proves not to be the case, those who follow nutrition guidelines will enjoy better health and put themselves at a lower risk for coronary heart disease and diabetes.

An aspect of nutrition that is *not* a matter of controversy is obesity, which is a subject of grave concern for all epidemiologists. That will be discussed in the last paragraph of this chapter.

BE PHYSICALLY ACTIVE

When I was young, we were not couch potatoes. What has changed in America to result in a generation of obese kids and their fat parents? My life many years ago may reveal a little of what has changed. As a boy, I had a bat made of wood and a ball. That was all it took to get a few kids out playing baseball. When not engaged in baseball (or football), we hurried to our bikes and covered many miles finding new territory to explore. We raked leaves, mowed lawns, and shoveled snow with muscle power. We walked to and from school. Many of us had paper routes—newspapers in those days were delivered on foot and on time. Desktop computers would not appear for another half century—so, there was no sitting watching figures move about on a small screen. I could go on and on, but the point is that exercise came naturally, and it was just what we did those many years ago.

Television was yet to come into homes, and junk food was either not available or we did not have the cash to buy it. I do not remember kids who were overweight. Clearly, we kept our caloric intake pretty much balanced with our energy output. This is *not* the case today. What is the solution? The American Cancer Society recommends exercise. I agree.

EXERCISE AND WEIGHT AFFECT MORE THAN CANCER RISK

Weight gain and reduced physical activity characterize our way of life in America. About two thirds of U.S. adults are overweight, and nearly a third of these are classified as obese, according to the World Health Organization. Obesity and lack of physical activity are associated with increased risk for cancer. What is the solution to this problem? The solution is simple enough: retain a healthy weight and get involved in exercise.

What is the incentive to watch weight and exercise? People who have occupations that involve daily physical activity have lower rates of colon cancer. Colon cancer is the third largest cancer killer in the United States. An expected 52,180 Americans will die of cancer of the colon and rectum in 2007, about three times the number of people expected to die of HIV/AIDS during the same period. I think that vigorous exercise is little enough to pay to reduce the possibility of colon cancer. A number of studies suggest that vigorous exercise reduces the risk of breast cancer, which is the second leading cause of cancer death to women in the United States. Again, exercise is a modest cost for reduced vulnerability to breast cancer. Men who have occupations that involve vigorous physical activity have a reduced risk for prostate cancer, which is the second leading cause of cancer deaths in men. Death is but one of the problems associated with prostate cancer. **Incontinence**, **erectile dysfunction**, fatigue, hot flashes, loss of **libido** also accompany prostate cancer. It is irrelevant whether these symptoms are due to the cancer *per se* or due to treatment. The problems are real—and enough to make me want to exercise now! Graham Colditz and Kathleen Yaus Wolin wrote in 2005: "A strong and consistent relation has been reported between obesity and mortality from *all cancers* [italics added] among men and women." Exercise makes one feel better—why not feel better and reduce the risk for a killer cancer at the same time.

There are health benefits other than cancer risk reduction with exercise, weight control, and a healthy lifestyle. There is now a "common agenda" for the American Cancer Society, the American Diabetes Association, and the American Heart Association. These health organizations seek to stimulate improvement in primary prevention for cancer, diabetes, and cardiovascular disease. Two-thirds of all deaths in the United States are due to these diseases. Yet prevention efforts are not well funded. Dr. Harmon Eyre and his associates wrote: "Despite the incontrovertible evidence supporting the medical and economic benefits of prevention and early detection, current disease control efforts are underfunded and fragmented."

A *DECREASED* LIFE EXPECTANCY IN THE NEW MILLENNIUM?

Life expectancy in the Western world has been gradually increasing for many hundreds of years. It is something that we have grown to expect. Many people are perhaps unaware that the amount of increase per unit time (decade or year or whatever) is now decreasing. The big increments in increased life expectancy were due to prevention of childhood diseases and more and better public health measures. Chapter 8 of this book chronicles diseases that were formerly rampant killers, but are no longer, at least to most citizens of the United States. So where are we going to get the extra years of life that accrue with enhanced life expectancy? Well quite frankly, it does *not* seem that we will have an increased life expectancy in the near future—and perhaps there may even be a *loss* in life expectancy in this big and rich country of ours. The important killers of today, cardiovascular disease, diabetes, and cancer are not going away in the near future. And what is ominous indeed is the fact that today's big killers may become even bigger killers. Why? Because of obesity.

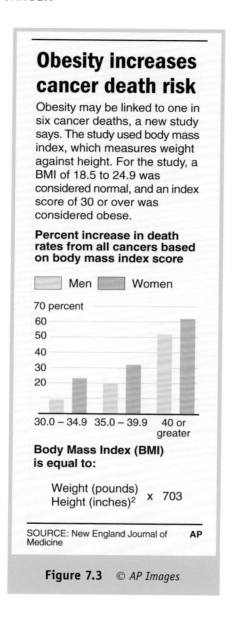

Obesity increases cancer death risk

Obesity may be linked to one in six cancer deaths, a new study says. The study used body mass index, which measures weight against height. For the study, a BMI of 18.5 to 24.9 was considered normal, and an index score of 30 or over was considered obese.

Percent increase in death rates from all cancers based on body mass index score

Men   Women

Body Mass Index (BMI) is equal to:

$$\frac{\text{Weight (pounds)}}{\text{Height (inches)}^2} \times 703$$

SOURCE: New England Journal of Medicine   AP

Figure 7.3 © *AP Images*

A potential decline in life expectancy is the subject of an important article in the March 17, 2005, issue of the prestigious *New England Journal of Medicine*. The source of the article is not listed to stimulate a mass run of high school students to the nearest medical library. Rather, the source is indicated to advise students that serious and thoughtful medical doctors and scientists view with alarm the epidemic of obesity and its effects on health and life expectancy. While this book is about preventing cancer, bear in mind that preventive measures for cancer apply to coronary heart disease and diabetes as well. Take home the message that exercise and proper diet will enhance the possibility of

---

◆ AMERICAN CANCER SOCIETY (ACS) GUIDELINES, 2005

The ACS states, and I concur, that "no diet can guarantee full protection against disease." The following recommendations were first published in 1984, reviewed in 1991, reviewed again in 1996, and were current as of September 2005.

1. Choose most of the foods you eat from plant sources
   ◆ Eat five or more servings of fruits and vegetables each day
   ◆ Eat other foods from plant sources, such as breads, cereals, grain products, rice, pasta, or beans several times each day
2. Limit your intake of high-fat foods, particularly from animal sources
   ◆ Choose foods low in fat
   ◆ Limit consumption of meats, especially high-fat meats
3. Be physically active: Achieve and maintain a healthy weight
   ◆ Be at least moderately active for 30 minutes or more on most days of the week
   ◆ Stay within your healthy weight range
4. Limit consumption of alcoholic beverages, if you drink at all.

a long and healthy life. The good doctors and scientists who wrote the 2005 article in the *New England Journal of Medicine* agree.

SUMMARY

The question of whether or not a proper diet can prevent cancer has no easy answer. What is clear is that a good diet and regular exercise have extensive health benefits and minimize the risk of numerous diseases. For the first time after many decades of rising life expectancy, people in the United States may be facing a decline in how long they can expect to live. This is due primarily to obesity. It is crucial to make a healthful diet and exercise a part of your life.

8

A FINAL WORD ON PREVENTION

KEY POINTS

♦ At least half of all, and probably much more, cancer diagnoses can be prevented.

♦ Far less money is spent preventing diseases than on treating them in the United States.

♦ History shows that many terrible diseases have been controlled or even eradicated through prevention.

"Despite the incontrovertible evidence supporting the medical and economic benefits of prevention and early detection, current disease control efforts are underfunded and fragmented."

Eyre, Kahn, and Robertson, 2004

". . . a conservative estimate is that at least half of all cancer deaths could in principle be avoided by the application of existing knowledge."

Cancer Prevention & Early Detection
Facts & Figures, 2005

The United States spends less than 3 percent of its total health budget on prevention studies—consider this in light of Secretary of Health and Human Services Margaret M. Heckler who, over two decades ago, gave voice to the notion of the simple truth that we can prevent most cancer. How long will it be before we believe Heckler's "simple fact," or the persuasive statement of the American Cancer Society, and do something about it? Governments may tarry but as individuals, we can endeavor to place ourselves and our loved ones at a reduced risk for cancer now. The readers of this book are urged to do just that.

Is a cure only a pill away? Most of us have gotten used to the idea that penicillin and the other "miracle" antibiotics can cure almost any disease and that it is simply a matter of time before cancer will be cured with a pill. As it is now, much cancer *is* cured—but at a cost. The cost includes damage to the individual who receives chemotherapy (see Chapter 5). Unquestionably, the cures are worth the profoundly powerful treatment. It is far better to have a survivor grandchild than one who ceases to live. Although Chapter 5 concerns survivors among young cancer patients, the painful lessons pertain to adults also. But would it not be preferred to prevent cancer in the first place?

A disease of self is a major part of the problem. Let us consider again the reference to penicillin and other antibiotics. Antibiotics are designed to kill invaders of the body. Example: The streptococcus bacteria group, which includes bacteria that cause scarlet fever and bacterial pneumonia. *Streptococci* are foreign to us. Their cells are constructed differently than are ours; for example streptococci have no nuclear membrane and they have a rigid cell wall. Beginning biology courses point out that human cells have nuclear membranes and no cell wall (a plasma membrane encloses our cells).

Differences in cell structure can be exploited to kill the invader (the bacteria) and not the host (the patient). Clever and immensely bright scientists have sought for differences in many of the pathogenic bacteria and have developed effective drugs that target the differences with the result that they are killers of noxious bacterial invaders. Penicillin interferes with the synthesis of a substance essential for cell wall formation. No cell wall results in bacterial death. Death not only for streptococci but also staphylococci, pneumococci, meningococci, and a number of other disease-causing organisms. However, because human cells lack a cell wall, human cells survive treatment with penicillin.

Contrast a bacterial invader with a human cancer cell: The cells of the cancer are the patient's own cells. Accordingly, the cancer cells have a distinct nuclear membrane as do all normal cells of the patient (with the notable exception of mature red blood cells, which lack a nucleus altogether). None of the cancer cells have a rigid cell wall, which of course is lacking in all normal host cells. One can go further and note that the cancer cells have mitochondria, cellular organs that power cells, as do all normal cells. The DNA of the cancer cell is *identical* to the DNA of normal body cells except for minute changes in the cancer cell DNA due to mutation or other genetic events. The list of similarities of cancer cells to normal cells could be extended to fill a textbook.

Now consider a drug that may become useful in treating cancer. It is likely that the drug, designed to kill cancer cells, will be toxic to normal cells as well. Without going into too much detail, consider cell division in cancer cells. They divide when they should not. Several chemotherapeutic agents have been designed to attack dividing cells. They work.

The dividing cells of the cancer will respond to the drug by not dividing. But unfortunately, so too will normal cells that are dividing—and these include the cells of hair follicles, the lining of the gut, and bone marrow where blood cells are made. With some chemotherapy, hair falls out, the gums bleed as do parts of the gut, and infection-fighting white blood cells drop in number. The reader already knows that not all cancer can be prevented (see Chapter 1). But *much* cancer can be prevented—there is no question it is much gentler to prevent than to cure. And cheaper, too.

Another problem is that cancer often works as a "silent" disease. Our bodies are wondrous indeed. We receive the gift of capacity greater than need. Our brains are competent to learn far more than we actually learn. We have excess kidney capacity and can survive with only one. We live with lungs that can exchange carbon dioxide with oxygen using only a small part of their capacity.

Why is excess capacity a problem? If a cancer begins to grow in the lungs, it may be years before it is detected. It grows "silently." The individual with a lung cancer feels no less well and experiences no difficulty in breathing for years. Those years of undetected cancer growth permits much time for metastasis to occur—without the patient even being aware that he or she harbors a malignancy. It is believed that metastasis occurs in at least 75 percent of cancer prior to detection. Metastasis is difficult to treat and metastasis often causes death. Again, prevention is far more preferable than the agony of treatment.

PREVENTION IS THE NAME OF THE GAME

My maternal grandparents' cemetery plot includes the graves of four children who died in early childhood during the latter part of the 19th century.

A similar situation is found in my paternal grandparents' cemetery plot. This is absolutely typical for the time. There have been no deaths among the offspring of my sibling and myself and our grandchildren. Why the difference? Prevention, not cure, of disease accounts for most of the lives saved. My children and my children's children did not have to endure and survive the diseases described below. There is a message here.

Diseases That Are Preventable in the Modern World

Smallpox.   Pandemic means that a disease is epidemic over a vast area and affects many people. Smallpox, aka variola, was pandemic in Western Europe in 1614, and only a few years later, it was epidemic in England. It was a leading cause of death at the time. Smallpox, an acute, often fatal, viral disease, was a scourge that elicited unsurpassed fear. Vaccination, developed initially by Edward Jenner (1749–1823), is credited for both prevention of the disease and the eradication of the pestilence. The last case in the United States was in 1949. The World Health Organization declared smallpox eradicated from the world in 1980. A specific treatment for this catastrophic lethal malady was never developed. Jenner did not cure—he *prevented* smallpox.

Cholera.   Cholera (see Chapter 1) is a gut infection caused by the bacterium *Vibrio cholerae*. The disease results in massive diarrhea of up to four gallons a day. Dehydration follows. Body temperature and blood pressure fall. Gut pain is so intense that, if the patient is not already in a coma, death is sought as relief from the illness. Death can occur within hours of infection. Cholera is still found in India and Southeast Asia, and it can occur in any country without basic sanitation. John Snow (1813–1858) discovered the mode of transmission of cholera prior to even knowing what it was in contaminated water that caused the disease. Snow discovered that cholera is spread by consumption of fecal-contaminated water and food. Many millions of lives in the United States have been saved by treatment of public water supplies that separate drinking water from sewage and which has been treated with chlorine to kill *Vibrio* and other pathogens. The utterly devastating lethal disease of cholera is not found where good public health measures are strictly enforced—treatment of water renders treatment of cholera patients unnecessary—by *prevention*.

Typhoid fever.   The bacterium *Salmonella typhi* causes this acute infectious disease. Fever of 104° to 105° is often followed by enlargement of the spleen and frequent bowel movements occur. These symptoms may be followed by twitching of the body, delirium, and a profound stupor. Fatalities are frequent. Clearly, typhoid is something to be avoided. It is spread by contaminated food and water. Filtration and chlorination of water supplies and other public health measures to ensure safe food have effectively *prevented* this noxious disease.

Measles.   Measles, aka rubeola, was a common, highly contagious, mostly childhood, viral disease. It formerly was a deadly disease but mortality declined in the twentieth century. A vaccine for its prevention was introduced in the late 1960s.

Typhus.   The Greek word *typhos* is the origin of our word typhus and translates as "stupor originating from a fever." Typhus refers to several acute infectious diseases including epidemic (louse-borne) typhus, scrub (mite-borne) typhus, and murine endemic (flea-borne) typhus. The different types have in common high fever, chills, terrible headaches, and ultimately delirium. Epidemic typhus has an especially high mortality rate. Epidemic typhus is caused by *Rickettsia prowazekii* transmitted by the bite of a louse. Similarly, the other typhus diseases are caused by bacteria transmitted through the bites of mites or fleas.

The insecticide DDT (dichlorodiphenyltrichloroethane) was used during World War II to kill lice and thus to prevent spread of epidemic typhus. DDT was also useful in containing plague, malaria, and yellow fever. Many people who fear the ecological effects of DDT forget the thousands (perhaps millions) of people whose lives were spared during World War II because of DDT. A thankful postwar world was pleased indeed that Paul Hermann Müller (1899–1965), the Swiss industrial chemist who developed a commercial process for the synthesis of DDT, was awarded the Nobel Prize in 1948. Cleanliness, in addition to the DDT, was absolutely necessary to prevent body lice. Probably few, if any, of the readers of this book personally know of anyone who has had epidemic typhus. The rule of thumb here is that no body lice means that typhus is *prevented*. DDT had an equally spectacular effect on malaria *prevention*—by controlling the mosquitoes that spread the disease.

Pellegra.   The term is derived from the Italian and means literally "rough skin." The disease was especially deadly in the southern United States where 100,000 deaths occurred in the first third of the 20th century. Pellagra's four "Ds" describe this devastating and deadly disease: dermatitis, diarrhea, dementia, and death. Pellagra has virtually disappeared due to the insight and hard work of Dr. Joseph Goldberger (1874–1929) of the United States Hygienic Laboratory (a predecessor of the National Institutes of Health). Goldberger showed that pellagra is not contagious and not caused by a virus or bacterium. It is caused poor diet. Pellegra is prevented by a diet of red meat, fish, beans, nuts, and whole wheat bread. That diet was shown by others to contain the water soluble vitamin niacin. No one is cured of pellagra with drugs. Pellagra is *prevented* by a well-balanced diet containing niacin.

Scurvy. This disease results in weakness, anemia, swollen and bleeding gums, loose teeth, great fatigue, and eventually death. Sailors were particularly vulnerable. The Scot James Lind (1716–1794) was determined to find the cause of death of sailors who died of scurvy in greater numbers than were lost in battle. He suspected it was due to their limited diet of bread and salted meat. Lind found that citrus

---

♦ THE PITIFUL PLIGHT OF YOUNG CHIMNEY SWEEPS

Percivall Pott was one of the first writers to describe a specific cancer, the cause of the cancer, the occupation group vulnerable for the cancer, and treatment for the cancer. In the London of 1775, Pott described scrotal cancer in clinical terms that are completely understandable to the modern reader. The scrotum is the bag or pouch of skin that contains the testes. Pott noted that chimney sweeps were more likely to have a skin cancer of the scrotum than other people. Further, he wrote that scrotal cancer "in these people [chimney sweeps], seems to derive its origin from a lodgment [i.e., the retention] of soot in rugae [rugae: wrinkles or folds of skin] of the scrotum.

Charles Dickens many years later described the plight of the English working classes. Pott was a near match to Dickens in writing about the difficulties of working people and perhaps social consciousness should be added to Pott's list of achievements. An example, taken from his scrotal cancer essay: "I never saw it under the age of puberty, which is, I suppose, one reason, why it is generally taken, both by patient and surgeon, for venereal. . . . The fate of these people seems singularly hard; in their early

fruits cured the disease and that lime juice added to the diet prevented scurvy. Lind published his report in 1753, and more than 40 years later, the British Navy ordered a daily dose of lime juice added to the diet, with the result that British sailors are known as "limeys" to this day. It was later learned that citrus fruits contain, among other things, vitamin C. It is the vitamin C that prevents scurvy. A bit of history: Only the

infancy, they are most frequently treated with great brutality, and almost starved with cold and hunger; they are thrust up narrow, and sometimes hot chimneys, where they are bruised, burned, and almost suffocated; and when they get to puberty, become peculiarly liable to a most noisome, painful, and fatal disease."

Pott was English and lived at a later time than the Italian Ramazzini (see Chapter 6) Yet, Pott knew of Ramazzini and referred to him in the context of occupational disease even though online indices (computer-generated bibliographic services—or Google for that matter) were not available in 1775. Ramazzini will be remembered for breast cancer and nuns; Pott will be remembered for scrotal cancer and chimney sweeps. Pott's never-to-be-forgotten chimney sweep cancer essay made possible behavior (bathing) that would *prevent* a loathsome and lethal cancer. The article on chimney sweep disease is only three pages long and is described in *The Surgical Works of Percivall Pott, 1775.*

Pott was born in London in 1714. At age 15 he became an apprentice for the study of surgery and by age 22 was admitted into the Company of Barber Surgeons. He became a distinguished surgeon with many famous patients and was knighted. Sir Percivall Pott died in 1788.

English ordered that citrus juice be added to the diet of their fighting men. During the American Civil War (1861–1865), United States and Confederate soldiers were dying of scurvy because of vitamin C deficiency. Note that drugs were not required to cure scurvy. A proper diet *prevented* the lethal disease.

Beriberi. Beriberi is found in Southeast Asia, including Sri Lanka. Beriberi in Sinhalese (the language of Sri Lanka) means "I cannot." The word refers to the totally wiped-out feeling and the inability, because of illness, to do anything. The disease involves inflammation of peripheral nerves, heart failure, edema, and diarrhea. It results from eating too much polished rice (white rice) in place of whole grains, nuts, pork, and fish. These other foods contain the B vitamin thiamin, which prevents beriberi. Eating foods containing adequate amounts of the thiamin *prevents* the beriberi.

Among the people to thank for many disease-prevention efforts are water treatment chemists who provide pathogen-free water and the plumbers who keep sewage and polluted water separated. Included also are the immunologists who fashion vaccines that prevent disease—and the epidemiologists who keep track of who gets a disease, where they live, their occupations, etc. These people are responsible for the prevention of many diseases and are, to a large extent, the reason why we enjoy an enhanced life expectancy.

Let's hope that cancer—or at least some cancers—can be added to the list of preventable diseases. For now, start by stopping smoking, staying out of the sun, protecting yourself against HPV, eating a balanced diet, and exercising.

SUMMARY

Too little effort is put into preventing cancer. Many forms of cancer can be prevented, yet most medical resources are spent in treating disease after it occurs. Historical efforts to wipe out or control diseases such as smallpox and typhus show that preventive approaches are effective. With so many of the risk factors for cancer subject to personal and lifestyle choices, it is important for individuals to make well-informed choices to improve their health and avoid unnecessary diseases.

GLOSSARY

◆

6-mercaptopurine (6-MP)   An anticancer drug that acts as a substitute for a normal precursor of DNA; this blocks DNA synthesis resulting in cell death. Elion and Hitchings received the Nobel Prize in 1988 for the development of 6-mercaptopurine.

acute lymphoblastic leukemia (ALL)   Malignancy of immature white blood cells, specifically activated lymphocytes. It is the most common acute leukemia of children. Acute refers to rapid onset and not long duration.

acute myeloid leukemia   A malignancy that usually occurs in adults characterized by proliferation of white blood cells of the bone marrow. Acute refers to rapid onset and not long duration.

AIDS   Acronym for acquired immunodeficiency syndrome; loss of immunity leaves the victim vulnerable to infection and some forms of cancer.

antibody   A molecule in the blood that tags, destroys, or neutralizes bacteria, viruses, or other harmful toxins.

antidepressant   A drug used in the treatment of severe feelings of gloom, hopelessness, sadness, and despair.

basal cell carcinoma   The most common skin cancer derived from the basal layer of epidermal skin cells. It is rarely metastatic and grows slowly. If not properly treated, it can become locally invasive with much tissue damage. It now afflicts young people although it formerly occurred primarily in older adults.

Bence Jones proteins Abnormal proteins found in the blood plasma and the urine in cases of multiple myeloma, named for Henry Bence Jones, an English physician (1813–1873).

busulfan An anticancer drug that reacts directly (binds with) DNA thereby blocking cell division.

cachexia Severe loss of weight.

carcinoma A cancer affecting epithelial *(q.v.)* cells.

celibate To abstain from marriage or sexual intercourse.

cervix Neck; when used as uterine cervix, the term refers to the portion of the uterus that opens into the vagina.

chemotherapeutic agent A chemical designed to cure a disease. In this book, it refers to drugs designed to cure cancer.

chlorambucil An anticancer drug known as a "nitrogen mustard" that acts to prevent cell division by binding with DNA.

cholera A disease of the small intestine caused by water or food contaminated with the bacterium *Vibrio cholerae*. It is often fatal because of vomiting and diarrhea.

chronic obstructive pulmonary disease (COPD) A persisting condition of airway blockage. Asthma and emphysema are examples.

cisplatin A platinum-containing anticancer agent that targets and binds with DNA to block cell division. It is considered curative in testicular cancer *(q.v.)*.

colposcope An instrument used for a magnified examination of the cervix.

colposcopy The examination of the cervix and vagina with a colposcope.

coronary heart disease   The coronary arteries supply the muscle of the heart with essential oxygen and nutrients. Coronary heart disease results in a decreased blood supply to the heart due to partial or complete blockage of one or more of the arteries.

corpus   A word meaning body; when used with uterus, the term refers to the main upper portion or body of the uterus; the isthmus connects the uterine corpus to the cervix (*q.v.*).

cyclophosphamide   An anticancer drug known as a "nitrogen mustard" which blocks cell division by binding with DNA.

cytologist   A person trained to detect changes from the normal in cells observed under the microscope.

cytotoxic   A term used with chemotherapy to indicate that the drug is toxic and probably lethal to cells.

endometrium   The term for the interior lining of the uterus. The lining consists of a single layer of epithelium, which covers a layer of connective tissue. The epithelium form glands that extend through the connective tissue to the muscular layer of the uterus. The epithelium, much of the glands, blood, and some of the connective tissue is lost during the monthly menstrual cycle. The young embryo attaches to (implants in) the endometrium if pregnancy occurs.

epidemiology   The science of the distribution and prevalence of disease.

epithelial   Epithelial cells cover the internal and external surfaces of the body and line hollow structures such as the gut. Epithelial cells form many glands.

erectile dysfunction   Inability to maintain a penile erection sufficient for sexual intercourse.

etiology   The cause(s) of a disease.

etoposide   A large molecule derived from podophylotoxin *(q.v.)* which blocks cell division by interfering with an essential enzyme.

fibrocystic   The term as used in breast disease refers to nonmalignant lumps in the breasts that vary with the monthly cycle. About one half of all sexually mature women have these nonmalignant lumps from time to time.

herpesvirus   A member of a large group of DNA-containing viruses that infect many kinds of animals and humans.

Hodgkin's disease   A cancer of lymph nodes, spleen, and other lymphoid tissue. The disease is named for the English doctor Thomas Hodgkin (1798–1866).

iatrogenic   Illness or adverse outcome of a disease caused by the physician. The word is derived from the Greek *iatros* meaning physician plus *genesis*, which means mode of origin.

immunosuppressive drugs   Drugs designed to block the immune response; generally given to patients after organ transplantation to prevent immune rejection of the transplanted organ.

incontinence   Inability to retain urine (or feces) voluntarily.

Jurassic   The second period of the Mesozoic era, about 200 to 150 million years ago, when giant reptiles dominated and birds first appeared.

leukemia   A type of cancer or malignancy that involves the white blood cells.

libido   Sex drive; loss of libido means loss of interest in sex.

lymphoma   Cancer involving the lymphocytes, or cells of the immune system.

malignant melanoma   A cancer of melanocytes, which are cells that produce the dark pigment melanin. The cancer is also known simply as melanoma. It occurs not only in the skin but may also occur in the eye, mouth, throat, anal canal, and other places.

mammography   The process of taking an X ray of the breast.

menstruation   The loss of blood and other material from the uterine lining that occurs about once per lunar month in women after the onset of puberty.

metabolic   The products resulting from the breaking down of substances by the body.

metastasis   Colonies of cancer cells that grow distant from the original cancer. Metastasis is unequivocal proof that a growth is cancer.

mortality   The number of deaths from a disease.

multiparous   The description of a woman who has borne more than one child.

multiple myeloma   A malignant tumor composed of plasma cells, which are ordinarily found in the bone marrow. The tumor cells will provoke the formation of characteristic multiple holes in bone.

mutant, mutations   A mutant is an organism that has undergone a change in its genetic material, the DNA. Mutations are permanent changes to the DNA that have occurred.

nanometers   One-billionth (10^{-9}) of a meter.

nasopharyngeal carcinoma   Cancer of the nose and pharynx, afflicting primarily males of China and other parts of southeast Asia. It is related in a causal way to a herpesvirus, among other factors.

nicotine   An important component of tobacco used as an agricultural insecticide. It is used in veterinary medicine to kill parasites. It is addictive similar to heroin and cocaine and is probably the major reason that it is difficult for smokers to quit.

non-Hodgkin lymphoma There are many kinds of lymphoma included in this term. Non-Hodgkin lymphomas (*q.v.*) are much more common than Hodgkin disease (*q.v.*). White blood cells known as lymphocytes divide without control resulting in enlarged lymph nodes in the neck, armpits, and groin.

nulliparous The description of a woman who has borne no children.

osteomas Non-malignant, slow growing, tumors of bone.

osteoporosis A loss of bone density with fractures that occur after minimal trauma; the condition is associated with the elderly, perhaps because of a decline in exercise and inadequate diet.

osteosarcomas Malignant bone cancers affecting primarily young adults.

paleopathology The branch of medicine dealing with ancient (fossil) disease.

papillomavirus Any of a number of viruses of the genus Papillomavirus. These viruses are found in many higher animals from birds to mammals including humans. All are characterized with DNA as genetic material. Genital warts and cervical cancer are caused by human papillomaviruses.

Pap smear Also known as Pap test. Named for George Nicholas Papanicolaou who developed a method for examination of exfoliated (detached) cells from the cervix as well as other organs. The exfoliated cells are placed on a slide, fixed and stained, and examined under the microscope for pathologic changes.

plasma cells Antibody-producing white blood cells.

podophylotoxin   A toxic compound obtained from the roots of the May apple whose scientific name is *Podophyllum*. The compound has several derivatives (etoposide, teniposide, *q.v.*) used in cancer therapy.

prospective study   An epidemiological study that starts with a population of normal (healthy) individuals and follows them to see what happens with respect to a particular disease. This is in contrast with retrospective studies that start with the diseased individual and endeavors to ascertain what led to the disease. Properly designed prospective studies are considered to have more validity than retrospective studies, which depend to a large extent on memory.

recidivism   Refers to resumption of an activity that was previously stopped.

retinoblastoma   A malignant cancer of childhood that occurs in one or both eyes. It occurs either due to heredity (genetically determined) or spontaneously.

sarcoma   A cancer of non-epithelial origin such as bone or muscle. Epithelial (*q.v.*) cancers, known as carcinomas (*q.v.*), are more common than sarcomas.

solarium   A room with one or more sun lamps for treatment with ultraviolet radiation.

squamous cell carcinoma   Second most common skin cancer after basal cell (*q.v.*) carcinoma. The cancer often has its origin in sun damaged skin of light complexioned individuals. Keratinizing cells (cells that turn horny and scale-like) of the skin form the cancer, which may become invasive and ultimately form metastases.

STD   Abbreviation for sexually transmitted disease.

solarium   A room with an ultraviolet light. These rooms were, and some still are, used to obtain a tan but medical experts no longer consider tanning healthy.

subsidy   Public funds to artificially keep the price of an item low.

teniposide   A large molecular weight derivative of podophylotoxin (*q.v.*) that is chemically similar to etoposide (*q.v.*) but is much more potent as an anticancer drug.

testicular cancer   The testis is the male germ cell (sex cell) producing organ. While children may have nonmalignant testicular growths, generally the tumors are malignant in adults.

transdermal   A method of administering a medication through the skin, such as the nicotine patch.

ultraviolet   Radiation with wave lengths shorter than visible violet light and longer than X ray.

vaccine   A substance that will assist the body in providing immunity against a disease; usually a weakened or killed virus or bacterial preparation, or an antigen derived from the virus or bacterium. The word is derived from the Latin *vaca* meaning cow because of the historic use of cowpox vaccine to prevent smallpox.

vibrio cholerae   Rod-shaped bacteria, found in the intestines of normal and diseased humans and in water, which cause Asiatic cholera. The bacteria are motile as indicated by the Latin *vibrare* which means to move rapidly.

Wilm's tumor   A kidney tumor of children that is rapidly growing and composed of embryonic tissues; it is also known as nephroblastoma.

FURTHER RESOURCES

◆

Bibliography

Abbasi, N.R., et al. "Early Diagnosis of Cutaneous Melanoma," *The Journal of the American Medical Association* 292(2004): 2771–2776.

American Cancer Society. *Cancer Prevention & Early Detection Facts & Figures 2005*. Atlanta: American Cancer Society, 2005.

Bendich, A., and R.J. Deckelbaum, eds. *Preventive Nutrition: The Comprehensive Guide for Health Professionals*, 3d ed. Totowa, N.J.: Humana Press, 2005.

Beral, V. "Collaborative Group on Hormonal Factors in Breast Cancer," *The Lancet* 360 (July 20, 2002): 187-195.

Bourdelais, Patrice. *Epidemics Laid Low: A History of What Happened in Rich Countries*. Translated by Bart K. Holland. Baltimore: The Johns Hopkins University Press, 2005.

Crawford, D. *The Invisible Enemy*. New York: Oxford University Press, 2000.

Crawford, D., and R.W. Jeffery, eds. *Obesity Prevention and Public Health*. New York: Oxford University Press, 2005.

D'Andrea, G.M. "Use of Antioxidants During Chemotherapy and Radiotherapy Should Be Avoided," *A Cancer Journal for Clinicians* 55 (2005): 319–321.

Hartmann, L.C., and C.L. Laprinzi. *Mayo Clinic Guide to Women's Cancers*. Rochester, Minn.: Mayo Clinic Health Information, 2005.

Hecht S.S., et al. "Similar Uptake of Lung Carcinogens of Regular, Light, and Ultralight Cigarettes," *Cancer Epidemiology Biomarkers and Prevention* 14 (2005): 693–698.

Hoh, Y.K., and H.K. Boo. "Prominent Women Biologists," *The American Biology Teacher* 65 (2003): 583–589.

Kluger, J. *Splendid Solution*. New York: Penguin, 2004.

Love, S.M. with L. Lindsey. *Dr. Susan Love's Breast Book,* 4th ed. Cambridge, Mass.: Da Capo Press, 2005.

McGinn, K.A., and P.J. Haylock. *Women's Cancers,* 3d ed. Alameda, Calif.: Hunter House, 2003.

McGrayne, S.B. "Portraits of Science. Damn the Torpedoes. Full Speed Ahead!" *Science* 296, 5569 (May 3, 2002): 851–852.

McKinnell, R.G., et al. *The Biological Basis of Cancer,* rev. ed. Cambridge, UK: Cambridge University Press, 2006.

Michalas S.P. "The Pap Test: George N. Papanicolaou (1883-1962), A Screening Test for the Prevention of Cancer of Uterine Cervix," *European Journal of Obstetrics & Gynecology and Reproductive Biology* 90 (2000): 135–138.

Milholland, R.B.R., and S.D. Hines. "Tobacco Induced Mutations: A Fun, Visually Impressive Experiment," *The American Biology Teacher* 66 (2004): 370–376.

Milne, Iain, and Iain Chalmers. "Documenting the Evidence: The Case of Scurvy." *Bulletin of the World Health Organization* 82 (2004): 791–796.

Okuyemi, K.S., et al. "Interventions to Facilitate Smoking Cessation," *American Family Physician* 74, 2 (July 15, 2006): 262–271.

Olshansky, S.J., et al. "A Potential Decline in Life Expectancy in the United States in the 21st Century: A Special Report," *New England Journal of Medicine* 352 (2005): 1138–1145.

Pott, Percival. *The Surgical Works of Percivall Pott*. London: L. Hawes, W. Clarke, and R. Collins, 1775.

Rockefeller University Press. *A Notable Career in Finding Out: Peyton Rous, 1879-1970*. Rockefeller University Occasional Paper 16. New York: Rockefeller University Press, 1971.

Rous, Peyton. "Transmission of a Malignant New Growth by Means of a Cell-free Filtrate," *A Cancer Journal for Clinicians* 22 (1972): 397–411.

Stephens, F. *The Cancer Prevention Manual.* Oxford, UK and New York: Oxford University Press, 2002.

Tulunay, O.E., et al. "Urinary Metabolites of a Tobacco-Specific Lung Carcinogen in Nonsmoking Hospitality Workers," *Cancer Epidemiology Biomarkers and Prevention* 14 (2005): 1283–1286.

Vilos, G.A. "Dr. George Papanicolaou and the Birth of the Pap Test." *Obstetrical and Gynecological Survey* 54 (1999): 481–483.

Watson, R.R., ed. *Functional Foods and Nutraceuticals in Cancer Prevention.* Ames, Iowa: Iowa State Press, 2003.

Wilds, J., and I. Harkey. *Alton Ochsner: Surgeon of the South.* Baton Rouge: Louisiana State University Press, 1990.

Web Sites

The Web sites that follow contain information about all of the subject matter contained in this book on prevention. The Web sites have been judged to contain authentic information about cancer and are easy to access.

American Cancer Society
http://www.cancer.org
> This is the Web site of The American Cancer Society (ACS) with an incredible array of useful information about smoking, prevention of cancer, early detection, treatment, and recent news.

Centers for Disease Control
http://www.cdc.gov/mmwr/
> This the address of the Morbidity and Mortality Weekly Report (MMWR), a weekly epidemiological digest for the United States published by the Centers for Disease Control (CDC).

Cancer Information Service
http://cis.nci.nih.gov
> The Cancer Information Service (CIS) contains information for smokers who wish to quit as well as cancer news, publications, and much more.

Harvard Center for Cancer Prevention

http://www.yourdiseaserisk.harvard.edu/

Search the Harvard Center for Cancer Prevention and calculate your risk of developing cancer.

Imaginis: The Breast Cancer Resource

http://imaginis.com/breasthealth/mammo_benefit-risk.asp

This Web site discusses the benefits and risks of mammography screening in detecting breast cancer.

Lance Armstrong Foundation

http://www.livestrong.org

LIVE**STRONG** is the name of the Web site of the Lance Armstrong Foundation, which has practical information and resources for cancer survivors.

Memorial Sloan-Kettering Cancer Center

http://www.mskcc.org

The Web site of the Memorial Sloan-Kettering Cancer Center of New York City contains information for about specific cancers, research, and up-to-date cancer news.

National Cancer Institute

http://www.nci.nih.gov

This Web site contains an almost inexhaustible source of cancer information provided by The National Cancer Institute (NCI). Learn about types of cancer, treatment, and screening.

Tobacco Free Kids

http://tobaccofreekids.org/reports/prices/

This site discusses the benefits of a rise in tobacco tax and how it can help deter people, especially teens, from smoking.

Tobacco Information and Prevention Source (TIPS)

http://www.cdc.gov/tobacco

This Web site has a plethora of information for people who wish to quit smoking. The site contains information on educational materials, tips for youth, and even celebrities against smoking.

INDEX

◆

ABOUT THE AUTHOR

♦

ROBERT G. MCKINNELL was born in Springfield, Missouri in 1926. He served in the United States Navy during World War II and the Korean War, attaining the rank of Lieutenant. He and his now deceased and beloved wife of many years, Beverly, are the parents of three children and the proud grandparents of five. He holds undergraduate degrees from the University of Notre Dame and Drury University, and a Ph.D. from the University of Minnesota. He was awarded a National Cancer Institute Predoctoral Fellowship while at Minnesota. Following Minnesota, he became a Postdoctoral Research Fellow at the Fox Chase Cancer Center, Philadelphia from 1958 to 1961. He taught and did cancer research for nine years at Newcomb College of Tulane University. He returned to Minnesota in 1970 where he was a professor of genetics and cell biology and was designated a Morse/Alumni Distinguished Professor. He became a professor emeritus in 1999. He was the 1981–1982 recipient of the Royal Society of London Guest Research Fellowship in the Nuffield Department of Pathology, Oxford University Medical School, Oxford, England. He received the Prince Hitachi Prize for Comparative Oncology awarded by the Japanese Foundation for Cancer Research, Tokyo, Japan, in 1998. He was a North Atlantic Treaty Organization (NATO) senior scientist, Department of Radiotherapy and Nuclear Medicine, Akademisch Ziekenhuis, Universiteit Gent, Belgium. He is a member of the University of Minnesota Cancer Center, the Minnesota Academy of Medicine and is an emeritus member of the American Association for Cancer Research and the American Association for Cancer Education. He is a past president of the International Society of Differentiation, Inc. He was a visiting scientist in the Industrial Medicine Department at Dow Chemical in Freeport, Texas. He has been the recipient of research grants from the American Cancer Society, Inc., the National Science Foundation, the National Cancer Institute, and the Damon Runyon Memorial Fund for Cancer Research, as well as a number of other research organizations. He has written several books on the subjects of cloning and cancer including (with others) *The Biological Basis of Cancer*, 2nd edition, 2006, Cambridge University Press. *The Biological Basis of Cancer* is also available in both Chinese and Japanese editions. He is the author or co-author of more than 100 articles published in scientific journals.